Mars Manderico
DESIGNER & ILLUSTRATOR

FROM POSSIBILITIES TO REALITY: SAVE YOUR SMALL TOWN
with these Uniquely Do-able Ideas, Projects, and Success Stories

Published by Deb Brown / Building Possibility

ISBN 979-8-218-44464-8

Forward

After spending nine years as co-founder of SaveYour.Town I've heard many stories, seen communities come together to create magic, and learned more from talking to rural people than I ever learned in school. I've been thinking about this book for a long time, and I'm thrilled you've found yourself reading this forward. Thank you for coming along for the ride.

THERE ARE EIGHT SECTIONS IN THIS BOOK:

These sections cover most rural topics I have seen in my work. There are chapters in each section that talk about a rural solution, tell success stories, and give you a space to create your own Idea Friendly projects.

Mary Redmond, a local newspaper editor and one of my beta readers, said about the following paragraph, "To me, this is the heart of the book. You've been there in the middle of this phenomenal experience countless times – and that's where the people picking up this book so want to be!!!!"

BUT THIS GATHERING WAS MORE THAN JUST A BRAINSTORMING SESSION. IT WAS A TESTAMENT TO THE POWER OF COMMUNITY ENGAGEMENT. AS THE CONVERSATION FLOWED, THE ROOM BUZZED WITH A SENSE OF UNITY AND SHARED PURPOSE. THE COMMUNITY MEMBERS DELVED INTO LOCAL ISSUES, GAINING A DEEPER UNDERSTANDING OF THEIR TOWN'S NEEDS AND POTENTIAL SOLUTIONS. THIS DIALOGUE FOSTERED A SENSE OF BELONGING, MAKING EACH INDIVIDUAL FEEL MORE INVESTED IN THEIR TOWN'S SUCCESS.

Rural communities are often neglected and we've had to learn how to take care of ourselves, to build the kind of communities we want to live in and raise our families in. This book shares some of those stories from rural places, and encourages you to continue to take care of your town too.

Thanks, Deb

Who should read this?

THE USUAL SUSPECTS:

Chambers, city managers, council members, Main Street people, economic developers – those people whose job responsibilities include some form of 'looking out for the town.'

BUT IT'S NOT JUST THOSE PEOPLE.

It's also the small-town community members, small business owners, entrepreneurs, non-profit organizations, church members, students, seniors and anyone who lives in a small town who wants to see change. You don't need to be licensed, degreed, or paid to create the community you want to live in. By supporting crafters, we can help them keep doing what they love and make the economy better.

WHAT MAKES THIS BOOK DIFFERENT?

This book is filled with stories of real rural communities and the work they've done. It's not a bunch of high-flying and costly ideas from a big-city intellectual with zero experience living in a small town. I'm in the trenches too. Many of these stories are ones I've helped along the way. All are from folks like you, who want to live in a place they can be a real part of and contribute to in a meaningful way.

SOME RURAL PEOPLE HAVE SAID TO ME, "WE JUST DON'T KNOW HOW TO GET STARTED AND MOVE FORWARD." THIS IS A BOOK OF POSSIBILITIES YOU CAN TRY OUT: FROM SMALL STEPS UP TO BIG PROJECTS.

It's a hands-on book that showcases completed projects, ideas from around the country, and encourages you to begin saving your own town. It's timely because no one is talking about this in a large way for small towns! You just can't be given big city ideas and be expected to dumb them down to solve your challenges. It is time to save your own towns and build community for all who live there!

How to use this workbook:

Easy. Peasy. Read it. Is there a story you like and might want to try in your town? Then invite some folks to join you, and just get started.

At the end of each section there's a page to get you started. Do that. **Begin the Idea Friendly** actions.

NO ONE EXPECTS YOU TO DO EVERYTHING, OR EVEN LIKE EVERYTHING! I GUARANTEE THERE ARE A FEW THINGS YOU WILL WANT TO START TOMORROW HAVE AT IT!

Questions once you get started? Email me! **deb@saveyour.town**

WHO AM I?

My work with small towns has taken me around the United States and Portugal, and I've been invited to speak virtually in Canada, Australia and New Zealand. I listen to what people tell me they'd like in their towns, and then help them take a small step towards testing that idea out. I share stories of other communities who are doing cool stuff, one small step at a time. I connect people to resources they might need, usually in their own communities.

THIS BOOK IS WRITTEN TO HELP YOU GET SOME IDEAS AND ENCOURAGEMENT ON HOW TO PURSUE YOUR BIG IDEAS!

EXCERPTS FROM OTHER WORKS NOTED IN TEXT.
PHOTOS BY DEB BROWN UNLESS OTHERWISE INDICATED.

THERE ARE 3 STEPS IN THE

Idea Friendly Method

Learn how to make your town more open to new ideas with the three-step Idea Friendly Method, created by my associate and collaborator Becky McCray. The Idea Friendly Method was created to be simple, easy to explain and quick to do. You don't need new committees and elaborate plans to accomplish your goals. You just need practical steps to put into action right away. Turn your big idea into a do-able, flexible approach that involves much more of the community in creating it together. Your situation is different from other towns. Customize any idea or any resource to make sure it will work for your community.

IT STARTS WITH YOUR BIG IDEA

1

Gather your crowd

Who wants to give your big idea a try? Who's interested in hearing more? Bring people together, but not at a meeting or through a committee. You might enjoy a cup of coffee with a couple of people and have a conversation about your big idea. Or work together on cleaning up a block in town and talk about what else you might do.

2

Build connections: Create a network of people who support the idea.

Your small group probably won't include expertise in all aspects of your big idea. No problem! Ask around. Who knows how to do this? Who knows how to do that? These connections might assist you for a short time, but they also might join your network for the long haul.

3

Take small steps: complete a miniature version of the idea first.

Want a new splash pad? Invite parents and their kids to your backyard. Set up the sprinklers. Ask the adults to bring their lawn chairs. Then see who comes. See if the kids like it and talk amongst the parents.

As you work your way through this book, consider how you can implement the Idea Friendly Method into each story and idea you like.

AND FINALLY ...

DON'T OVER-ANALYZE. DON'T LOOK FOR THE REASONS IT WON'T WORK. DON'T HAVE BORING MEETINGS. JUST GET STARTED ... AND HAVE FUN.

LET'S GET TO WORK!

In this workbook you are encouraged to use the Idea Friendly Method. It begins with your Big Idea. I want you to think: **"What do we want to see in our town?"**

Write a few things down here.

_____

_____

_____

_____

_____

_____

_____

_____

_____

_____

_____

_____

_____

_____

_____

_____

_____

_____

_____

_____

_____

_____

An Idea Friendly Story from a Small Town

Mila Besich, mayor of Superior, Arizona shared a note with Becky and me about how they are using the Idea Friendly Method. I love the top ten rules they use!

WE LOVE FOLLOWING YOUR BLOG AND VIDEOS HERE IN SUPERIOR, AZ. OUR COMMUNITY IS SMALL, 3,068 RESIDENTS, LESS THAN TWO SQUARE MILES. WE HAVE MANY CHALLENGES AND HAVE HAD ALL SORTS OF INTERNAL CONFLICTS. YOU CAN DO A GOOGLE SEARCH ABOUT SOME OF OUR ISSUES, WE ARE AN EXAMPLE OF HOW ANY COMMUNITY CAN OVERCOME THOSE CONFLICTS.

In 2016, an election took place and soon after that election we convened a community retreat with our Town Council, School Board, Chamber of Commerce and our newly formed 501(c)3 Rebuild Superior Inc. The focus of the discussion: how could we all work together to build our community?

We wanted to share some of our ideas with your readers on how we have stayed idea friendly. This is mostly an attitude and philosophy but has proven to be helpful for our success. Most importantly, don't be afraid to dream big and communicate as often as you can with everyone.

We had two issues we wanted to tackle up front. Blight and Youth Retention. We did not have a huge budget for either special program but we committed $10,000 for blight and $5,000 for a Youth Leadership program. It was a start, and both programs are making significant impact. We also did not over study either program.

Here's our Top Ten rules on how we try to run things from inside Town Hall.

1. **Always keep an open door** and be willing to help individual citizens solve their problems.

2. **Support community giving organizations** through non-financial means, such as using the influence of Town leadership to support events.

3. **Make town facilities available** and optimized for community programs as cheaply as possible.

4. **Participate in and honor the contributions of community organizations.**

5. **Always be willing to do what you can** (within the rules) for your fellow man.

6. When you find an ordinance or policy that is unfair, don't **be afraid to change** it.

7. **Look for ways you can work with other groups** and individuals for positive change.

8. **Be willing to take a back seat to others ideas,** do not insist on complete control and be open to putting time and resources behind those ideas.

9. **Insist that all code and zoning reviews are completed in a timely manner,** with no backlogs or waiting lists. This makes expedited permits unnecessary.

10. **Look for ways to say yes.** Things that are impossible as written may be possible with a simple change of approach know the code well enough to be able to navigate the customer through that process.

KEEP UP THE GREAT WORK THAT YOU ARE DOING. THANKS FOR THE INSPIRATIONS.

— Mila Besich

Bring People Together

SMALL TOWNS GATHER FOR MANY REASONS.

Opportunities to gather encourage residents of small towns to interact, build relationships, and feel a sense of belonging to the community. This strengthens the social fabric.

Gathering places like cafes, parks, and community centers draw people downtown, generating foot traffic and economic activity for local shops and restaurants.

Community gatherings allow small towns to preserve and showcase their unique cultural heritage through events, performances, and shared experiences.

INCLUSIVE GATHERING SPACES AND EVENTS HELP BRING TOGETHER PEOPLE OF DIFFERENT BACKGROUNDS, INCOMES, AND AGES WITHIN THE SMALL TOWN COMMUNITY.

GATHERING IS ESSENTIAL FOR THE VITALITY AND RESILIENCE OF SMALL TOWN LIFE.

Coffee and Calendars

PARTNER TO COMPARE CALENDARS

Invite the nonprofits and organizations that plan activities to an hour or two of Coffee and Calendars. Hold this gathering in a comfortable location with tables where people can spread out. Provide coffee! Ask them to bring their calendars.

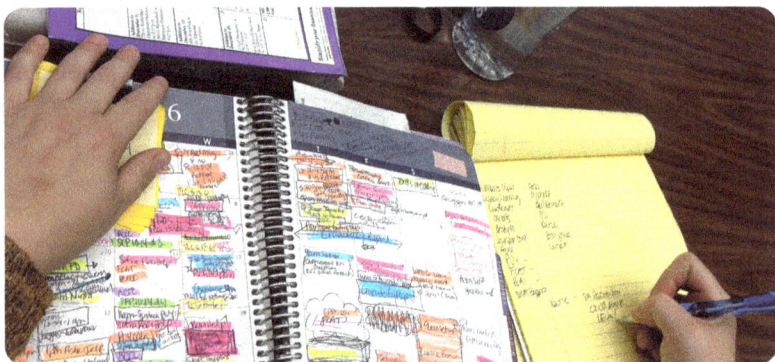

You'll find out things about the organizations you didn't know. You'll figure out how to create a day full of events, instead of a day with events happening all at the same time. Coming together helps to build community.

We did this when I was a chamber director in Webster City, Iowa. We had about ten non-profit people at our first gathering. I thought we knew pretty much everything there was to know about each organization. Boy, was I wrong! **Each person had the opportunity to talk about what they did for the community, what they needed to be successful and share what they were planning.** One example of a project I didn't know anything about came from Building Families. They had a funding program to help people who wanted to have a daycare from their home. Funding to fence in the yard, get their state licensing, and other small items they might need to bring their home up to code.

Don't tie yourself to just nonprofits. Your businesses could do this too. It's a great activity to do quarterly to prepare for the next quarter. Learn to work together to promote each other, and that starts by sharing what you do with others.

Success Stories:

WALL, SOUTH DAKOTA POPULATION 695

Wall held a "Coffee and Calendars" event. Cheyenne said, "The event was a success! About ten community members joined the meeting, shared their calendars, and enjoyed coffee and conversation. This was a community need that is now filled. We look forward to more "Coffee and Calendar" events and continued community collaboration."

RINGGOLD COUNTY, IOWA POPULATION 4,670

Jodie, the Ringgold County, Iowa Development director told us they hosted two cookies and calendar meetings. One was for town representatives and one for the Mount Ayr retail businesses. The town reps wanted to meet again. That's a sign they thought it was worth their time! The retailers met and planned dates for the ladies' night out events for the entire year. Normally, this is done sporadically, with not enough communication.

Jodie also started a Google doc for each group to communicate within their groups. She's finding out that the younger people don't read email!

BE IDEA FRIENDLY: GATHER YOUR CROWD, BUILD CONNECTIONS, TAKE SMALL STEPS

- In all three stories, the Gather Your Crowd portion was bringing different groups together: nonprofits in Webster City, ten community members in Wall and town representatives and retailers in Ringgold County.

- Building Connections happened when the non-profits got to introduce themselves and talk about what their places of work offered. Many people didn't know about the child care option in the one business.

- Taking Small Steps was emphasized well in Ringgold County when the retailers made the simple decision to choose dates for their ladies night out events.

TAKE NOTES HERE

- **Who are the people you work with regularly?** Start with the organizations and companies who have events that might align with your work. Make a list.

- **Invite them for coffee.** Have them bring their calendars too. Have each organization tell the others what they do and share something they might not know about. This allows everyone in the room to give better referrals to those organizations!

- **Then look at your calendars to see if there is an opportunity to partner together on an event.**

Becky and I have started doing this Coffee and Calendars with our peers and partners, and meeting virtually for Coffee and Zoom. It's great to catch up, share news and activities and perhaps collaborate in unique ways.

_____

_____

_____

_____

CHECK IN:

What connections did you build? What worked and what didn't?
What small step will you/your crowd take and when?

_____

_____

_____

Industrial Businesses Need to Gather

Success Story | MINERVA, OHIO | POPULATION 3,700

As you gather people together, don't forget your larger businesses. Don't assume they meet regularly, or even that they know each other. In 2019, I went to Minerva, Ohio, for an on-site visit. At one of the gatherings we brought together the various CEOs and leaders of the industrial businesses. It was held at one of the businesses in their lunchroom and yes, we had food! There's an old saying, "we don't meet if we don't eat." I think that came from a rural community! The Chamber director and a person from the city came with me. This gathering started out like a meeting, but by bringing in food and having light conversation over lunch it became more relaxed.

I ASKED THE OTHER TOWN REPRESENTATIVES TO LEAVE THE ROOM AFTER WE ATE.

The space needed to be filled with peers in their industry. This gathering was not about promotion or marketing, it was about building bridges and connecting with each other. Then we began an interesting discussion.

I ASKED EACH PERSON TO TELL ME WHO THEY ARE AND WHAT THEY MANUFACTURE AND TELL ME WHAT THEY WANT FOR MINERVA.

It started off a little shaky, only because the first person had never really been asked what he wanted for his town. Once we cleared that up, all of us learned a lot about each other that we did not know.

One owner said that he needed more space for his business and was having trouble finding it and worried he'd have to leave town. Another business owner quickly answered, "I have space you can use." They went on to create a partnership still in effect today that has helped to strengthen both businesses.

THEY AGREED TO HELP CREATE BETTER COORDINATION WITH THE COMMUNITY COMING TOGETHER. AND TO OFFER LESS RESISTANCE TO CHANGE TO DO BIGGER THINGS, STARTING WITH THEMSELVES.

They were all in agreement they needed better transportation to move goods out into the world. They also found out they had similar ideas about other projects, and they had the opportunity to network with each other. This had not been done before!

BE IDEA FRIENDLY: GATHER YOUR CROWD, BUILD CONNECTIONS, TAKE SMALL STEPS

The industrial businesses were gathered by the Chamber director. They built connections easily when discussing what their business did and what they might need. Small steps happened when they began talking with each other about better coordination for bringing the community together.

TAKE NOTES HERE

What group of industrial, manufacturing and small scale manufacturing businesses could you bring together? Would you want to try it with service businesses? Start a list for each.

_____

_____

_____

_____

_____

_____

_____

_____

_____

_____

CHECK IN:

What connections did you build? What worked and what didn't?
What small step will you/your crowd take and when?

_____

_____

_____

_____

_____

Dig Deeper
ASK PEOPLE WHAT THEY WANT

Success Story | JACKSON COUNTY, KENTUCKY | POPULATION 13,000

In one small county in Kentucky, I met with a group of people who had been invited to hear from the expert (that was me). I don't come in and lecture people. I don't know what they want for their towns! One such meeting was held in an old historical building now being used as the office of Backroads of Appalachia. Through motorsports-focused tourism, they work to drive economic development and opportunity in the poverty-stricken areas of Appalachia. Lots of people attended. I think they expected me to tell them how to save their town.

What we did was gather around and have a conversation. I started by asking them what they wanted. Either personally, business-wise or for their community. Kathy, a local property owner and involved resident was sitting next to me. She had this idea to provide tourists with different forms of transport, such as ATVs and other recreational vehicles, to use for a fee. She owned one side-by-side, and wondered if that was enough to get started. Yes! It's a small step, and a great way to try your idea out. Will people want to rent that vehicle? How much should you charge? What about insurance? These are just a few of the questions you can answer more easily if you are taking small steps. Several people chimed in and had suggestions for her and offered to donate canoes, bicycles and other means of transportation for her to use.

We went around the room, heard what someone else wanted, and visited about it.

YOU'LL HEAR ME SAY THE WORD 'VISIT' A LOT IN THIS BOOK, INSTEAD OF THE WORD 'TALK'. I THINK VISITING IS A MORE RELAXED WAY OF TALKING WITH SOMEONE, AND IT ALSO MEANS HEARING EACH OTHER IN THE CONVERSATION. IT'S FRIENDLIER AND MORE WELCOMING.

Gathering Together Creates Magic

But this gathering was more than just a brainstorming session. It was a testament to the power of community engagement. As the conversation flowed, the room buzzed with a sense of unity and shared purpose. The community members delved into local issues, gaining a deeper understanding of their town's needs and potential solutions. This dialogue fostered a sense of belonging, making each individual feel more invested in their town's success. One thing we learned was there are 58 different lodging places in the county as potential partners. This was a surprise to many in the room, and opened up even more conversation about partnering with each other around the different opportunities.

What happens when you bring people together to talk about their town and their needs?

• increased **community engagement** (people talking to one another),

• greater **understanding and civil discussion** of local issues,

• and the **creation of solutions** that many people can work on.

Kathy (left), a resident of Jackson County, Kentucky, chats with visitors

THIS TYPE OF CONVERSATION ALSO HELPS INDIVIDUALS FEEL MORE INVESTED IN THE SUCCESS OF THEIR TOWN.

SECTION 1 | BRING PEOPLE TOGETHER

BE IDEA FRIENDLY: GATHER YOUR CROWD, BUILD CONNECTIONS, TAKE SMALL STEPS

From Kathy's story you can see her big idea was to provide transportation for recreational activities. We gathered a crowd of folks who wanted to do things for their county, like Kathy did. They knew of some other folks who wanted to help (build connections). The small steps started with Kathy talking to the lady who offered the canoe!

Everybody brings something to the table, even if they may not know what that is yet. There is magic in the discovery that happens when people can just talk through an idea/dream in a safe space, and before you know it, people are offering up suggestions, connections to people they know, and resources to help solve the underlying problem.

TAKE NOTES HERE

Who do you know that likes your big idea, that thing you want to see in your town, that event you'd like to hold, that dream for your area? **Make a list of those people now.**

Then invite them to visit about it. *"Hey, I've got this idea for our town I'd like to run by you. Let's go for coffee (or a beer, or dinner, or to my house) and let me tell you what I'm thinking."* It's not a committee meeting. It won't be for everyone. It's just a few folks getting together to hear about your idea.

18 FROM POSSIBILITIES TO REALITY | SAVE YOUR SMALL TOWN

CHECK IN:

- What connections did you build?
- What worked and what didn't?
- What small step did you or will you take? When?

_____

_____

_____

_____

_____

_____

_____

_____

_____

_____

_____

_____

_____

_____

Links:

- Backroads of Appalachia: https://backroadsofappalachia.org/
- Jackson County, Kentucky and Grayson, Kentucky, stories of volunteers:
  https://buildingpossibility.com/articles/jackson-county-and-grayson-ky-stories-and-volunteers/

Tools from SaveYour.Town:

- If you're looking for someone to help make this happen, it's one of the things
  SaveYour.Town does during an 3 Day Community Engagement Idea Friendly visit.
  This is a product we offer for purchase.
- Details here: https://buildingpossibility.com/services/3 Day Community Engagement-visits/

Community

In rural places, community holds a distinct significance –
it is shared values, mutual support and relationships with
longtime friends and family.

THE FABRIC OF A RURAL COMMUNITY IS WOVEN THROUGH VARIOUS ACTIVITIES SUCH AS LOCAL EVENTS, VOLUNTEER WORK, AND COMMUNAL GATHERINGS, FOSTERING A SENSE OF BELONGING AND TOGETHERNESS.

This bond is further strengthened by the reliance on one another
for various needs, be it economic, social, or emotional. The
community members often come together to address common
challenges, celebrate traditions, and preserve local heritage.

ALSO, RURAL COMMUNITIES TEND TO HAVE A STRONG CONNECTION TO THE SURROUNDING NATURAL ENVIRONMENT, FURTHER SHAPING THEIR IDENTITY AND WAY OF LIFE.

YOU CAN ACCOMPLISH MORE THINGS WITH MORE PEOPLE. PEOPLE REALLY DO WANT TO HELP.

THEY DON'T WANT TO:

- Attend endless meetings.
- Be required to volunteer for years at a time.
- Be stuck in a boardroom making decisions (and then have nothing happen).
- Be responsible for huge projects and deal with the committee of negativity.

NOW THEY CAN DO THINGS IN A NEW WAY. THEY CAN HELP IN SMALL BUT MEANINGFUL WAYS, AS A COMMUNITY.

Build a Library of Things.

Success Story | AKRON, IOWA | POPULATION 1,540

I like the idea of organizations coming together and collaborating, instead of always working in silos. How could you test out this idea in a practical way in your small town?

Most of our minds, when we hear about creating a library of things, go right to the actual library. And we know that libraries are a great place for people to come together – people of all generations, capabilities, ways of thinking. But how can a library of things be a way of convening and collaborating for people and organizations?

A library of things is a location for things you rarely use. The community donates the things and people can use them by checking them out. These items are things like tools, sewing kits or sewing machines, artsy things, electronics, gardening things, and so on.

The old way of thinking about a project of this is to assemble a committee of non-profit organization leaders and let them be in charge. They will gather and vote on the best ideas and determine, as a committee, what kind of library of things is needed in your community. There are a few problems with that way of doing things. First of all, who has time to serve on committees? Traditionally, those folks are already overworked. Often they are part of the STP, the Same Ten People.

What if you just started with a group of people who would like to do this kind of project?

In Akron, Iowa, the retired farmers had moved into town and brought along their woodworking equipment. They put the tools in their garages, until the wives suggested strongly that they move those tools somewhere else. This group of farmers met every morning for coffee at an old hospital no longer in use. Being curious individuals, they explored that building and realized there was a dry basement.

THEY THOUGHT THE BASEMENT OF THAT BUILDING WOULD BE A GREAT SPACE FOR ALL OF THEM TO BRING THEIR WOODWORKING MATERIALS AND TOOLS. THEY GOT THE PROPER PERMISSION AND DID JUST THAT.

Their goal was to be available to anyone who wanted to learn how to use the tools and make things. They now work with the shop teacher at the high school and students. They have helped locals try a project before investing in their own equipment. And they also make things for the community, like the signs at the edge of town that welcome visitors. Is this convening or collaborating to better serve your community around a targeted purpose? Yes! These retirees are now more active in the community and see more possibilities of how they can serve. It's how they found out about the need for new signage at the edge of town.

THEY CREATED A LIBRARY OF THINGS AROUND WOODWORKING.

BE IDEA FRIENDLY: GATHER YOUR CROWD, BUILD CONNECTIONS, TAKE SMALL STEPS

In Akron, the wives motivated the men to gather their crowd! They built connections by talking with the shop teacher. They first took small steps to make sure the basement was dry.

Who do you know in your town that might want to gather their crowd?

_____

_____

_____

_____

_____

_____

_____

_____

_____

_____

_____

CHECK IN:

What connections did you build? What worked and what didn't?
What small step will you/your crowd take and when?

_____

_____

_____

_____

Fix Up Your Parks

WHO IS RESPONSIBLE FOR YOUR PARKS? IS IT YOU?

Many rural places I travel have natural resources, trails, and fun recreational things to do. You are no different. But what I do notice is that rural folks don't recognize all they do have!

Folks have said they want more things to do (for all ages). They want to make their parks even better. You could use history as a place for tourists to have some fun. That could be a historical trail for people to follow like the Bozeman Trail in Montana or a story walk about the local historical figures like libraries do. What about tours of older buildings and places like railroad depots, early settler housing or underground railroad locations. Every small place will have its own few historical connections.

MAKE YOUR PARKS EVEN BETTER.

How could you create small groups of park ninjas? Ninjas are those folks who slide in, do the work unobtrusively, and slide out. Trim edges, pull weeds, clean statues – and it could be adults and students! They could paint picnic tables, build new ones, repair, or even build a new overhead shelter! Getting our kids invested in these kinds of projects is the kind of work you want them to do. It also commits them to our community and helps bring them back.

I live in Gulfport, Mississippi, population 72,000, and just read a comment on Facebook, "Why is there so much trash on the beach?". One person said, "Just pick up what's around you. It takes a few minutes. Do your part."

THAT'S A GREAT FIRST STEP.

HOW CAN CITIZENS HELP TO FIX UP PARKS?

Pick up trash with your friends, and have fun doing it.

Organize educational events and workshops in the park. I attended a foraging event in one of my local parks. Two people who forage and use the goods to create tinctures decided to share their knowledge. They posted on Facebook "Come learn foraging with us' ' and asked people to pay $25 each. All I had to do was show up at the park! There were over 20 people who came. It was an afternoon of learning about foraging where I lived, meeting new people and getting my steps in.

Encourage the use of sustainable practices, such as composting and reducing plastic waste, within the park. Hold a workshop showing how to compost. Many municipalities supply compost for residents to pick up. Compost acts like a sponge for water and helps produce nitrogen, phosphorus and other micronutrients needed for plants to grow. Check with your local city or county officials. There are also many sites online that can teach you how to make your own compost.

BE IDEA FRIENDLY: GATHER YOUR CROWD, BUILD CONNECTIONS, TAKE SMALL STEPS

Think about your parks. What would you and your crowd like to see happen, your big idea?

Now, what are some small steps you can take towards accomplishing that big idea? I'm a fan of easy and small steps. Foraging is a good fit, and you could partner with your local extension people or county or Department of Natural Resources people.

This picture is a park in Letcher County, Kentucky – they planted wildflowers and created a natural selfie shot location!

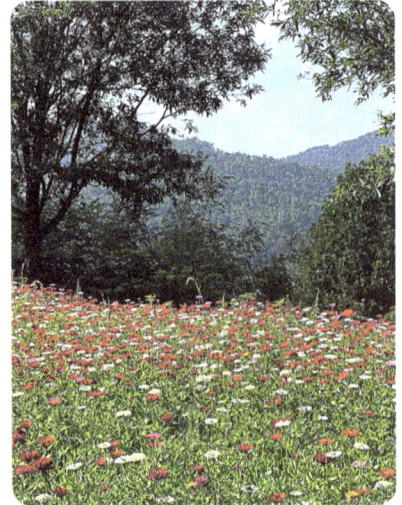

CHECK IN:

What connections did you build? What worked and what didn't? What small step will you/your crowd take and when?

Municipal compost from garbage projects:

https://theconversation.com/city-compost-programs-turn-garbage-into-black-gold-that-boosts-food-security-and-social-justice-136169

Invite the Community To Plan Events

LEAVE ROOM FOR OTHERS

I have a secret about how to make events even more successful.

DON'T PLAN THEM ALL OUT.

If you do all the planning, the only choice you give people is whether they should come or not. Instead, leave room for locals to do some things. I had to plan a big event for a 12-hour day. Instead of planning it all out, I just asked people what they wanted to do. Then I put them in charge of that. Just that.

One guy wanted a chili cookoff. I said, "Go for it, and here's your spot". A local youth group wanted to bring their human foosball game to the event. Of course, we said yes!

THE SECRET IS IF YOU LET PEOPLE BE A PART OF THE FUN WITH WHAT THEY WANT TO DO, THEY BRING THEIR FAMILY AND FRIENDS WITH THEM!

WHAT KIND OF ACTIVITIES COULD YOU HAVE AT A STREET PARTY?

- live music performances
- food vendors
- carnival games
- face painting
- a photo booth

- a community art project
- a scavenger hunt
- local talent showcase
- historical or cultural exhibits

The key to a successful street party event is to create a fun, inclusive atmosphere that celebrates the unique character and culture of your town.

MAKE SURE YOU DON'T PLAN IT ALL YOURSELF!

Ask people what they want to do at a street party, then let them do it!

Photo by Deb Brown at RVTV

AN IDEA FRIENDLY STORY FROM A SMALL TOWN

Hello from freezing Battle Lake, Minnesota! Thank you so much for writing about your winter woes. It's hard to rally the troops and stay motivated as the temperature drops. I wanted to share with you that last winter, my partner and I had the most out of state winter visitors we've ever had and it instilled a sense of pride in our ability to live on the tundra. We took our Texan, Oregonian, NYC friends ice fishing, snowshoeing, and were reminded how much we really don't get out and do stuff!

For some reason last year opportunities kept arising in the winter months and some of my favorite events to date happened when it was minus 30. I think it's a good reminder to just keep brewing up ideas and planning for fun events that people can brag about how tough and awesome they are because they live in a place where you can drive on a frozen lake!

It's CRAZY...people come from all over the world because the lake in the middle of our town often has the best ice for sailing at this time of the year. So fun! Check this site out for cool pics! https://www.iceboat.org

BE IDEA FRIENDLY: GATHER YOUR CROWD, BUILD CONNECTIONS, TAKE SMALL STEPS

Try this in your next event. **Ask people what they want to see included in the event.** Dig, really listen to what they say. Be sure to ask students! Then give the space to do it, encourage them, be helpful – **but let them do it!**

CHECK IN:

What connections did you build? What worked and what didn't?
What small step will you/your crowd take and when?

Why New Residents Are Moving to Rural Areas

IT'S ALL ABOUT THE INTANGIBLE BENEFITS OF LIVING THERE.

WHY DO PEOPLE WANT TO MOVE TO SMALL TOWNS AND RURAL AREAS?

- a slower pace of life,
- a stronger sense of community,
- a lower cost of living,
- more access to nature,
- to be closer to family,
- to be a big fish in a small pond.

HOW CAN YOU PROMOTE QUALITY OF LIFE IN YOUR TOWN?

First of all, find out what people who live in your town already value. Why have they stayed? What are the good things about your town? You could start by asking these questions on social media. Then start a list. Perhaps create it in a shared document and encourage people to add to the list.

I did this. We had a photojournalist come to town and he was paid to talk about what was NOT working. And he did, including pictures. It was in *The New York Times*. It ticked me off. So, I asked people…. What were the new businesses? What new activities were happening? I then wrote a rebuttal and sent it off to the Times. And they printed it.

That kicked off a barrage of activity and a ton of pride in our town. Because of that article, SquareUp came to town and made a movie about the closing of the factory.

Continue to promote your town. Take small steps. Get people talking about the positive things happening in town. Every time you hear a good story, share it with at least one friend. Or post it on social media. Or tell the local paper and radio station the story. And encourage your crowd to do the same.

BE IDEA FRIENDLY: GATHER YOUR CROWD, BUILD CONNECTIONS, TAKE SMALL STEPS

Stop listening to the committee of negativity. What kind of easy process can you create to share the good stories?

Let many people be involved in that activity. In the olden days (of course I've only heard about this second-hand!) when something needed to be done, one person would call another on their phone tree list. And that person called another on their list. And so on. Duplicate that – but online! O.K. – where will you start?

CHECK IN:

What connections did you build? What worked and what didn't?
What small step will you/your crowd take and when?

Links:

• **Rebuttal to the** *New York Times:*
  https://buildingpossibility.com/articles/rebuttal-to-the-new-york-times/
• **See the film Made in Iowa:** https://squareup.com/us/en/dreams

Dig Deeper

MONTANA BUILDS A COMMUNITY

Success Story | THE BOZEMAN TRAIL

I spent two years on a community-building project in SE Montana. This was a collaboration between folks in the five counties I worked in with the purpose of building community across the region. We didn't know at the beginning of the project what "community" would look like. We just knew we had to bring all kinds of folks together and let them determine what their focus would be.

STEVE AND MIKE HAD THIS IDEA WE COULD DO SOMETHING AROUND THE HISTORY OF THE BOZEMAN TRAIL. THE TRAIL CUTS ACROSS ALL FIVE COUNTIES.

We began putting together lists of people who might be interested. We started with twelve folks from museums, city and state office workers, historical re-enactors, researchers, Crow tribal people, and retired folks. Zoom calls were organized and they brought to light the need for a map of the Bozeman Trail that could be used to create projects for the counties.

There were no deadlines. We weren't involved in this project to be efficient. It was important that all the voices were heard, and everyone was encouraged to try their ideas out.

Several in the group began working on a physical map of the Bozeman Trail. Penny had a makeshift map in her county museum and that was a good starting point.

The Zoom calls happened about every month at first. Some of the action steps taken early on were:

• Mike shared his videos and photos of the Trail.

• Several people worked on access points in each county.

• We wrote support letters for Mike's related project.

• We began posting on social media and sharing with others about this group.

THERE WAS NO ONE PERSON IN CHARGE. IT WAS CHAOTIC. AND IT WAS EXCITING! PEOPLE WANTED TO BE INVOLVED AND WERE THRILLED THAT THEIR VOICES MATTERED.

Some of the folks that joined in along the way included:

• Patrick from the Absaroka-Beartooth Wilderness Foundation and Brendan from Columbus bringing GIS digital mapping capabilities with them.

• Ralph, local trail mapping expert.

• Lucas, Professor at Rocky State University and his college students.

These professionals went to work with their sleeves rolled up and began the process of mapmaking.

Many adventures were enjoyed

The Crow tribe has their lands in several of the counties. Rose Williamson, a local Crow artist and storyteller of the Battle of Little Big Horn from the viewpoint of the Crow, joined the process. Several of us participated in her virtual Airbnb experience.

ROSE TOLD THE STORY OF THE CROW AND LITTLE BIG HORN VIA AN ONLINE LIVE PRESENTATION. SHE ENTHRALLED US ALL. ROSE ALSO GAVE AN IN-PERSON TOUR OF THE HAYFIELD BATTLE AREA.

She told stories of what happened and all of us walked the area and imagined what life was like back then along the trail. A visit to Howard Boggus, Crow historian, was arranged. Howard and Mike have walked parts of the trail together and Howard has walked it all. Howard has a basement full of Crow history, including much about the Bozeman Trail.

A word from a town like yours ...
Deb Brown has assisted the Beartooth RC&D region in Montana with targeted economic recovery efforts. Deb's experience and expertise in working with Chambers of Commerce and small businesses has hastened our regional economic recovery efforts.

I find Deb Brown to be engaging with the communities we serve and willing to share ideas that have been successful elsewhere. Taking small steps and trying something new or different aren't easy concepts for every business to grasp. Deb's encouragement to tourism and travel-impacted areas has been most helpful.

Sincerely,
Executive Director Steve Simonson,
Beartooth Resource Conservation & Development Area, Inc., Joliet, Montana

DEB'S ENCOURAGEMENT TO TOURISM AND TRAVEL-IMPACTED AREAS HAS BEEN MOST HELPFUL

Some other adventures included:

TRAVELING THE TRAIL

- A visit to Bill Yellowtail's land to see where he believes the trail came through.
- Some have walked the trail and some have done research (and continue to do so.)

TELLING THE STORIES

- I videotaped: Howard telling some stories, Steve and Mike sharing talk of the Bozeman Trail, and Doc telling trail stories.
- Several group members spoke at the Wyoming and Montana legislature, and presented in various locations whenever asked.
- Raymond, Chamber Director from Big Timber, Montana, population 1,662, explored the stories along the trail in his town. There are hot springs along the trail; John Bozeman was killed in this area and Greycliff Mill is on the trail. Raymond also fixed the Google listing that says synagogue Bozeman trail. There was no synagogue.

LOCAL INVOLVEMENT

- Stephanie, Economic Development Director in Columbus, Montana, population 1,903, worked with locals to paint the street for Absarokee Days in the summer.
- The former mayor, current mayor, and some biz owners from Joliet , Montana, population 609, have beautified the main street. There's a Bozeman trail river crossing on a piece of land the city owns, and a chuck wagon on the main road they are decorating.
- The EDA from Billings, Montana, population 120,000, considered various locations for signage and kiosks: Coulson Park and Blue Creek fishing access site is another crossing for the tribes and the trail people probably camped there.
- The museum people have created displays, answered a ton of questions, and go along on some of the in-person trail visits.

2024 IS THE 160TH ANNIVERSARY OF THE BOZEMAN TRAIL. THE FIVE COUNTIES ARE PLANNING MANY ACTIVITIES AND A WALK/RIDE OF THE TRAIL.

RALPH SAID, "I'VE ENJOYED EVERY BIT OF THIS – IT MIGHT BE KEEPING ME ALIVE."

This is just another reason we wanted to do the Bozeman Project as a collaborative effort. Because it matters to so many people that are involved. It's not a committee deciding what is important and what steps need to be taken. It's people who want to be involved in sharing the story of the Bozeman Trail and finding ways to claim and promote their part of the trail. Each small step anyone takes adds to the value of the Trail. Even if they never reach a specific "finished" state. It is a living project and anyone or any group can be involved.

BE IDEA FRIENDLY: GATHER YOUR CROWD, BUILD CONNECTIONS, TAKE SMALL STEPS

Thinking about creating a large project that people want to get involved in is mind-numbing. So don't do that. Instead bring people you know together and ask about their ideas of what community could be. Make a list of those people now.

_____

_____

_____

_____

_____

_____

_____

_____

_____

_____

_____

_____

CHECK IN:

- What connections did you build?
- What worked and what didn't?
- What small step did you or will you take? When?

Youth and Young Families

Why do we decide our youth have no say in our small towns? We know they are active in sports. We know they are smart; they achieve accolades for honor society and the like.

Now it is time to realize they can play a big part in our small towns – if we allow and encourage them to.

We have all heard "There's nothing to do here." Hanging out is an opportunity to learn to be with others, share ideas, be creative, and support each other. Is there that opportunity in your community?

CONSIDER THAT ALL THE YOUTH ARE PART OF YOUR COMMUNITY. NOT JUST THE ATHLETES AND SMART ONES. HOW ARE YOU ENCOURAGING THEM TO BE MORE INVOLVED?

When a group of students builds benches in shop class and then places them around town, they are contributing to the community. They are also building pride in their town. They will remember years from now how they created something valuable for their neighbors.

What other ways can they contribute? Let them try their ideas. Don't micromanage. They are your future leaders.

Youth Involvement

START WITH THE ARTS

Consider the younger years as the time when they get to experiment with and explore the arts. They learn how to collaborate with others while working on art together, to develop their problem-solving skills when devising art projects, and to better use critical thinking to help tell their cultural stories. They are not as tied up in team sports, and can participate in dance class, a book club, or a painting workshop, for example.

As children age, after-school activities grow too.

HOW DOES A COMMUNITY MAKE IT POSSIBLE FOR MIDDLE AND HIGH SCHOOL STUDENTS TO STAY INVOLVED?

Meet them where they are. **Stop waiting for them to come to you.** Involve them in student-driven art projects in the town.

- The welding class could design and make benches to be placed around town.
- Design students could create drawings for projects like murals, sculptures, and painted streets and crosswalks.
- Art classes could hold exhibitions in empty buildings.
- Engage both art and shop students to design and make "Selfie Stations".

It's a perfect marriage to join empty buildings and art together! Use your empty buildings to showcase your art. They did it in Athens, Pennsylvania, population 3,265. Here's what they said:

"Last summer we used a vacant store, put out a registration via JotForm, and had a great show. We organized a street fair to celebrate the completion of our first mural, closed the street, and had live music. There were so many people in the street having fun. It was very successful and over 400 people came inside to see the art! The building that housed the show was vacant and for sale. The building owner was happy to have so many people through the building."

IN RURAL AREAS, OUR CULTURAL ARTS ARE OFTEN EXPRESSED THROUGH MUSIC, CRAFT, FOOD, AND WAYS OF DOING THINGS.

These are things all of us do. We don't think of it as 'art'. But it is, and it helps make our communities stronger when we can connect through these various skills. And that means all of us, from youth to seniors.

BE IDEA FRIENDLY: GATHER YOUR CROWD, BUILD CONNECTIONS, TAKE SMALL STEPS

What are some of the different cultural foods in your town? Invite those cooks and some students to come together and talk about food as art. How can the shop students meet and create art? Or the agriculture groups?

_____

_____

_____

_____

_____

_____

_____

_____

_____

_____

_____

CHECK IN:

What connections did you build? What worked and what didn't?
What small step will you/your crowd take and when?

_____

_____

_____

_____

_____

Links:

- Use Art to build community: https://saveyour.town/use-art-to-build-community/
- Athens, Pennsylvania art: https://buildingpossibility.com/articles/art-and-empty-buildings/

Involve Your Students

AND LET THEM LEAD

It's important that your youth are heard. We know when a student is involved with a project, such as building benches, painting, or other beautification efforts, they see what community means. This also builds a positive connection to their town.

The young man who helped build a bench that goes downtown will tell you 30 years later, "I helped make that bench." This involvement in their community helps bring them back when they are adults.

Students know how to participate in school activities, now you also want them to take part in your community. Help them take pride in your town, listen to their ideas, and try out their ideas in an Idea Friendly way. Value students' input and energy.

TIPS ON GETTING YOUNG PEOPLE INVOLVED

Let them experience your business. Don't just preach at a one-day event and talk about what you do. Bring them onsite for half a day. Let them work with you, either by job shadowing or paying them to help in your business.

- Tony Guidroz, from San Saba, Texas, population 3,127, told us he was shocked when he found out there were 702 kids in the local school district, and more than 400 were considered "at-risk" either because of grades or language barriers. Tony wanted to give them more choices and more chances. So, he shared his idea for a Blue Collar Career Fair.

- He brought heavy equipment operators, an HVAC contractor, a stone mason, a plumber, an electrician, and a welder, all to one location for hands-on demonstrations. The kids could try their own hands at moving some dirt, burning some metal, or stripping some wire. Tony's hope is to grab the attention of some kids who haven't thought about these high-paying local jobs that are in high demand, but don't require four years of college.

You see the new mindset at work here: rather than employers letting grades or language barriers stop kids from applying, they're connecting directly.

Students are asked to volunteer at events. **Ask them what they'd like to do at your event. Then let them do it.** (It's how I found out about Human Foosball, by allowing students to install their own idea at a Chamber event.)

- **Ask them to create a placemaking project that benefits your town.** Build public benches, create art like murals or painting the street, paint rocks and place around town for people to find – there are lots of ideas they can try.

BE IDEA FRIENDLY: GATHER YOUR CROWD, BUILD CONNECTIONS, TAKE SMALL STEPS

Do you know your students? Where do they hang out? Go there. (coffee shop, Taco Bell, sporting events, etc.) Ask them what they want in town. **And don't tell them no.** I did that in Paulding, Ohio. I told a group of students that Taco Bell was not a good idea. Five years later a group in that town made it possible to bring Taco Bell in as a new business!

CHECK IN:

What connections did you build? What worked and what didn't?
What small step will you/your crowd take and when?

Support High School Entrepreneurs

Success Story | NORFOLK COUNTY, ONTARIO | POPULATION 64,000

One terrific youth entrepreneurship program happens in Norfolk County, Ontario. They have a summer project for kids in grades 6 through 12, called the Student Start Up project, or SSUP.

Kids can apply for real money to start a real business. They submit a quite simple explanation of what business they want to start, following an elementary level "business plan" template. Over the years Norfolk County has offered anywhere from $50 to $200 in start-up grants to the kids, depending on how much funding is available.

Then kids run their businesses all summer. And during the summer, Norfolk County holds a special marketplace event, where the young entrepreneurs can feature their businesses in booths and displays. I'm sure people in the county look forward to this every year.

AT THE END OF THE SUMMER, KIDS CAN EARN A SMALL CASH BONUS BY TURNING IN A FINAL REPORT THAT LOOKS A LOT LIKE A SIMPLE PROFIT AND LOSS STATEMENT.

Photo courtesy of Norfolk County

WHAT ARE SOME ENTREPRENEURIAL PROJECTS HIGH SCHOOL STUDENTS ARE DOING IN SSUP?

- a local **delivery service**
- **handmade crafts** to sell at farmers markets or online
- **lawn care or pet care** services
- a **tutoring or music lesson** business
- a **social media management company** for small businesses in the area

BE IDEA FRIENDLY: GATHER YOUR CROWD, BUILD CONNECTIONS, TAKE SMALL STEPS

Does your high school have an entrepreneurial class? Introduce yourself to the teacher! Find some small ways you can be involved. When our movie theater closed, a group of us decided to save it. One thing we did was work with the entrepreneurial class and they created movie trailers for us! They also named our organization HERO – help entertain and restore organization. Can you find future entrepreneurs through those who are leaders in 4-H, Junior Achievement and other local groups. Where will you start?

CHECK IN:

What connections did you build? What worked and what didn't?
What small step will you/your crowd take and when?

SSUP: https://www.norfolkcounty.ca/news/student-start-up-program-ssup-enjoys-another-great-year/

Your Students Want Places To Eat

TACO BELL LEADS THE WAY IN REQUESTS

The students almost always say they want a Taco Bell. Don't tell them no! Instead start with a trial run. Declare Taco Tuesday, have them shop, make the food, learn the value of the products, and learn how to be a good salesperson. Let them do the math, figure out what to buy, make the promotional pieces and create $5 meal deals. Finally, feed everyone. Whether they can afford it or not. Let the kids learn the value of giving, too.

It's easier than you think. Let the students lead the way and try out their ideas for testing the idea of Taco Tuesday. Some things they'll need:

- ideas for who might donate to the cost of food.
- location for this venture.
- recipes for tacos and how to expand those recipes to serve and sell to a lot of people.
- some instructions from people who sell at the farmers markets on how to be a better salesperson.

Your job is NOT to tell them what to do. Your job is to listen to their ideas and offer suggestions if asked. Or bring in someone new who might be able to help them. Involve as many people as possible. And have fun!

WHAT ARE SOME WAYS TO TEST IDEAS FOR A NEW EATING PLACE?

- **Host a pop-up event** to give potential customers a taste of what you have in mind.
- **Use a community kitchen** to try recipes and sell food.
- **Ask a local church if you can cook in their kitchen** and host an event for them with your food.
- **Try a 'sample night'** and give away food.

PROMOTE YOUR NEW IDEA AND PROJECT!

- **Attend local food festivals** to network and get more ideas.
- **Reach out to local food bloggers** and influencers to attend.
- **Utilize social media** to gather feedback and engage with potential customers.
- **Partner with local businesses** to cross promote your idea, set up in their lot or in front of their store.

BE IDEA FRIENDLY: GATHER YOUR CROWD, BUILD CONNECTIONS, TAKE SMALL STEPS

HERE'S SOME SMALL STEP IDEAS:

Some schools have youth cooking classes, eat there. Invite a student to attend a cooking class with you. Check out TikTok and see what youth are doing around the idea of creating food places. Who is always in the kitchen?

CHECK IN:

What connections did you build? What worked and what didn't?
What small step did you/your crowd take and when?

Don't Forget the Former Youth Who Moved Back Home With Families

FIND THEM!

People are moving back to their small hometowns, bringing their work and young families with them. Do you know who they are?

We've heard for decades about the "brain drain" of young people graduating and leaving small towns, but we are not noticing a significant return of young adults. It is easy to miss because we don't have anything like a graduation ceremony to draw our attention to our "Brain Gain" families.

Dr. Ben Winchester, a rural sociologist with the University of Minnesota, found that these 30 to 44-year-olds arrive with college degrees, years of experience in the workplace, and large professional networks. Often, they are families with young children, boosting rural school enrollments. **Sometimes, they pick a small community they have never lived in before, representing a recruiting opportunity.**

Younger families today are choosing where they want to live first and finding their work second. Frequently, they find it online or start their own businesses. Ben says there are three reasons young people 30-44 move to rural communities: a slower pace of life, safety and security, and the low cost of housing.

So, if you focus on creating jobs to help recruit new residents, you're missing the key motivators.

HOW DO YOU FIND THOSE PEOPLE WHO WANT TO START A BUSINESS AND MOVE TO YOUR AREA?

- **Look at sites like Kickstarter and Etsy,** and you'll likely find entrepreneurs already in your area.

- **Join online communities** or forums related to entrepreneurship, work from home, or the industry gaps you're looking for entrepreneurs to fill.

- **Use social media platforms** like LinkedIn, Facebook, Instagram, TikTok, or Threads to network with and find entrepreneurs, join groups, and participate in discussions.

SOME OF THESE FOLKS ARE ALREADY IN YOUR TOWN AND HAVE ENTREPRENEURIAL BUSINESSES!

Reach out to them in a couple of ways:

- **Attend local or virtual events,** workshops, or conferences related to entrepreneurship or your industry. You can meet other business owners, exchange ideas, and learn from experts.

- **Consider visiting a coworking space** or a business incubator in your area. You can find other entrepreneurs, hear their stories, see what resources they are being exposed to, and attend their events.

BE IDEA FRIENDLY: GATHER YOUR CROWD, BUILD CONNECTIONS, TAKE SMALL STEPS

Who did you find on Kickstarter and Etsy? Search in a 50 mile radius. Who's already doing something? Make that list. Then work with your crowd and start connecting to these people. The goal is to build a relationship. Invite them for coffee. Ask how you can help them. Remember, small steps.

CHECK IN:

What connections did you build? What worked and what didn't?
What small steps do you/your crowd take and when?

Ben Winchester: https://extension.umn.edu/contacts-community-development/ben-winchester

Dig Deeper

ADD YOUNG PEOPLE TO YOUR CITY COUNCIL

Their say matters too.

Why not add a non-voting student to your city council? What a wonderful way to get insight from young people. And it doesn't have to be just to the city council.

IN RESEARCHING THIS TOPIC, I FOUND A GRAPHIC NOVEL THAT TELLS THE STORY OF SEVERAL STUDENTS WHO SERVED IN A GROUP IN WASHINGTON FOCUSED ON PLANNING. IT DAWNED ON ME THAT THE OPPORTUNITIES WE PRESENT TO STUDENTS ARE OUR IDEAS. NOT THEIRS. I WOULDN'T HAVE CONSIDERED USING A GRAPHIC NOVEL TO TELL A STORY.

American Planning Association Washington Chapter, Youth In Planning Task Force – Aims to encourage youth to get involved in local planning initiatives. Tools include the Washington By and By graphic novel and examples of youth engagement in planning initiatives across the state.

Photo from Brett Jordan on Unsplash

Why does it matter?

Voice and Participation — Involvement in local government allows students to have a voice, be heard, and participate in decision-making processes that affect their community

Inspiring Others — Student involvement can inspire others to join and be part of the initiative, leading to a more engaged and representative local government

Community Ownership and Impact — It allows students to make a difference in their community, address local issues, and contribute to causes that matter to them

Influence on Schools — Local politics often dictate what happens in schools, and student involvement can influence these decisions

Career and Employment Opportunities — Involvement in local government can lead to employment opportunities and valuable connections

Overall, being on the local city council enables students to make a tangible impact on their community, gain valuable experience, and contribute to the democratic process.

HOW DO I ADD HIGH SCHOOL STUDENTS TO MY CITY COUNCIL?

- **Research the requirements for city council membership** and see if there are any provisions for adding student representatives.
- **Reach out to local school officials** or student groups to gauge interest and gather support.
- **Check with your school administration** to see if they have any existing partnerships or relationships with the city council.
- **Research the backgrounds of current city council members** to see if any of them have previously served as student representatives. Then talk to them!
- **Attend city council meetings** as a spectator to get a sense of the issues and topics that are being discussed. This can help you better understand the role of a student member.
- **Reach out to other local youth organizations,** such as the YMCA, 4H or Boys and Girls Club, to see if they have any programs or initiatives related to civic engagement or leadership development.

BE IDEA FRIENDLY: GATHER YOUR CROWD, BUILD CONNECTIONS, TAKE SMALL STEPS

Start by talking to youth. It could be in a more formal setting, like a presentation at the school. Or it could be at the local coffee shop after school. What kind of questions did they ask? What was the interest level? Who else could you ask to join you in the endeavor?

CHECK IN:

- What connections did you build?
- What worked and what didn't?
- What small step will you/your crowd take and when?

Links:

- Youth in planning taskforce:
  https://www.washington-apa.org/youth-in-planning
- Washington by and by:
  https://apawa.memberclicks.net/assets/docs/Youth_In_Planning/WashingtonByandBy/
  WashingtonByandBy_forscreenviewing.pdf
- Examples of Youth Engagement: https://www.washington-apa.org/yip---planners

Art As Economic Development

Is art economic development? Yes, it is.

BUSINESSES ARE OFTEN ATTRACTED TO COMMUNITIES WITH A VIBRANT ARTS AND CULTURE SCENE. THIS IS BECAUSE THE ARTS CAN HELP TO ATTRACT AND RETAIN TALENT, AND THEY CAN ALSO CONTRIBUTE TO A CITY'S OVERALL QUALITY OF LIFE.

The arts and culture sector generates billions of dollars in tax revenue each year. Production of arts and cultural goods and services in the U.S. added 4.3 percent directly to the nation's GDP in 2019, for a total approaching a trillion dollars ($919.7 billion).

This amount remains greater than the value added by such industries as construction, transportation and warehousing, mining, and agriculture.

This revenue can be used to support public services, such as education and infrastructure. The arts can help to promote tourism in a community. Visitors are often drawn to cities and towns with a variety of cultural attractions, such as museums, theaters, and festivals.

Public Art: Anyone Can Do It!

Success Story | HARMON, OKLAHOMA | POPULATION 2,428

Residents want more places to sit downtown. I hear this at most of my Three Day Community Engagement visits to small towns. They also express interest in seeing original art in the crosswalks and as murals on downtown buildings. You can find examples of this all over the internet. You want people to begin brainstorming about how art could be incorporated into the public life of the community, perhaps using local history as inspiration.

Photo by Harmon County Forward in Hollis, Oklahoma

Harmon, Oklahoma, shared this image of snowflakes in an empty window. How easy is that to do? You could partner young students with seniors to make the snowflakes and put them in the window of an empty building. Perhaps you're having a Christmas in July celebration. Wouldn't it be fun to see these in all the empty buildings?

HOW TO GET PEOPLE INVOLVED IN CREATING PUBLIC ART

Make it possible for every resident, no matter his/her age or ability, to participate in some way.

Why couldn't the county residents cut out paper snowflakes and put them inside every empty building in town? Better yet, have the students learn how to make snowflakes with your seniors!

Don't stop there. Take a ton of pictures and post them everywhere. Write a press release and send it to every paper in the state. **MAKE IT A BIG DEAL.**

ART PROJECTS ANYONE CAN DO

- **Have a block party that features local artists.** A dance class could perform. You could make art with chalk in the driveways, have a mini concert on a front porch with singers in your town, or invite the community theater to perform a scene from their latest production. Get the schools involved by giving art teachers space for a gallery showing students' work. **Don't do all the planning yourself.** Ask your neighbors what they want to do and then encourage them to do it.

- **Make a list of current public art and sculptures.** Give readers a brief backstory of each piece, in addition to its location. Share that info on social media.

- Take some pictures and **create a walking trail.**

- **Paint rocks** and place them around town. People can take one as long as they replace it with another one.

- **Decorate chain link fences** with bottle caps.

BE IDEA FRIENDLY: GATHER YOUR CROWD, BUILD CONNECTIONS, TAKE SMALL STEPS

Try out an art project with your friends (ideas above or create your own.) Be sure to have fun! Share the story everywhere. I know I didn't mention anything about public music, perhaps you could bring together a few folks to play music!

CHECK IN:

What connections did you build? What worked and what didn't?
What small step will you/your crowd take and when?

Statistics by state:

https://nasaa-arts.org/nasaa_research/creative-economy-state-profiles/

Make It Easy and Temporary

LET EVERYONE PLAY

A mural might be out of your community's budget, but that doesn't mean you can't take small, artistic steps. A great medium is colored chalk.

Start on the sidewalk. Or a blank side of a building. Do you have a bare spot or two on an existing mural? Fill in the space with chalk. Turn a blank, boring retaining wall into a colorful spot.

Divide up downtown. Recruit a diverse crowd. Have kids come after school to color on the sidewalks. When your canvas washes off after a few rains, the pressure is off to create a masterpiece. That empowers people who wouldn't otherwise participate in an art project to get involved. And, before the rain comes, the murals will generate interest and conversation around creating more art.

WHAT ARE SOME PUBLIC ART IDEAS USING CHALK?

• Inspirational quotes or messages to brighten people's day.

• Interactive games, such as hopscotch or tic-tac-toe.

• Nature scenes that promote environmental awareness and appreciation.

• Pictures of your pets.

• Ask the participants what they want to do!

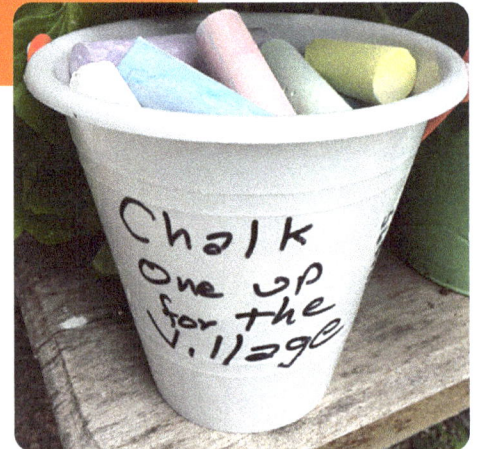

I GAVE BUCKETS LIKE THESE TO THE VENDORS ON OUR FRONT ST. IT WAS MY CANADA DAY (JULY 1) PROJECT. ALSO, I HAVE HAD SUCCESS IN USING SIDEWALK CHALK IN SHOWING OFF MY NEW ANTIQUE QUILT STORE! I DRAW QUILT SQUARES AND ARROWS TO THE FRONT OF OUR BNB.

– Marian Langhus
Village of Gagetown, New Brunswick | Canada, population 711

BE IDEA FRIENDLY: GATHER YOUR CROWD, BUILD CONNECTIONS, TAKE SMALL STEPS

Do you own a business in town? Connect with other business owners on your block and have a chalking event! Invite kids to come downtown and create designs on your sidewalks with chalk. There are many ways to organize this, go for the easiest!

CHECK IN:

What connections did you build? What worked and what didn't?
What small step will you/your crowd take and when?

Create an Outdoor Museum

OLD CARS, FARM EQUIPMENT ARE JUST TWO IDEAS

Don't let the word "museum" throw you off. There's nothing stuffy about these ideas. Fun, whimsical, and free to visitors is the way to go. It could be anything! Consider this "carhenge" in Alliance, Nebraska, population 8,037.

The tourism director in Jackson County, Kentucky pondered this idea and realized that by asking those folks that have junk cars in their yard to make art out of it solves two problems. It brings more art to town. And it helps with the old cars trashing up the neighborhood. Ask those who have junk cars in their yard if you could have them. What creative things could you do with them?

How about a tractor graveyard? What weather-resistant or happily rusty artifacts would tell the story of your town?

HOW COULD YOU WORK WITH PEOPLE WHO HAVE THESE RELICS IN THEIR YARDS TO CREATE ART?

OLD CARS IN THE BLACK HILLS

Take a look at the site Black Hills Hiking and Biking and More – they've dedicated a page to old cars in the Black Hills. I think these VWs would make a great outdoor museum!

WHAT KIND OF OUTDOOR MUSEUMS COULD BE CREATED IN AN EMPTY LOT?

Sculpture gardens, historical reenactment sites, botanical gardens or art installations all could be used to dress up an empty lot. The possibilities are endless. Consider:

- **A nature preserve.** Start small. Create a birdwatching station. Plant local flora and add signage to tell what it is. Benches, swings or other seating are a great add-on.
- **A music garden.** An outdoor museum that celebrates music includes musical instruments that visitors can play. Make the museum spot a welcoming place for local musicians to perform. Make a stage out of pallets. Could your local shop classes help?
- **A tiny farm.** An outdoor museum that focuses on sustainable agriculture could be a great way to teach people about growing their own food. It could include raised garden beds, workshops on composting and organic gardening, and even a farmers market.

BE IDEA FRIENDLY: GATHER YOUR CROWD, BUILD CONNECTIONS, TAKE SMALL STEPS

An open-air museum is a great idea for rural communities! If it were me, I'd go to the local veterans' club and ask them to help make their own kind of museum idea happen.
Who are you going to talk to?

_____

_____

_____

_____

_____

_____

_____

_____

_____

CHECK IN:

What connections did you build? What worked and what didn't?
What small step will you/your crowd take and when?

_____

_____

_____

_____

_____

Links and photos:

- Carhenge: https://carhenge.com/
- Black Hills Hiking and biking:
  https://www.blackhillshikingbikingandmore.com/old-cars-in-the-black-hills

SECTION 4 | ART AS ECONOMIC DEVELOPMENT

Make Seating

AND IT DOESN'T ALWAYS HAVE TO BE MATCHING

Make benches. This is an art piece made out of an old propane tank by artist Tim Adams. Who could do that in your towns? Or ask the shop class to design and make benches for downtown. A town could just budget the money and buy benches from the standard bench place. Then they would be more uniform. Maybe it will last longer.

But how does that build community? Things don't always have to match. Involving local artists, students and just regular folks gets the community involved. There is a piece of ownership in it.

MAKE IT A PROJECT WHERE MANY PEOPLE CAN BE INVOLVED, IN LARGE AND SMALL WAYS. HAVE SOME FUN.

Photo by Deb Brown featuring work of Tim Adams

WHAT ARE SOME DIFFERENT WAYS TO MAKE PUBLIC SEATING?

- **Install benches** in public areas such as parks, sidewalks, and community centers.
- **Create seating areas using recycled materials** like wooden pallets, cinder blocks, and tree stumps.
- **Use existing structures** such as walls and ledges to create seating areas.
- **Partner with local businesses** to install seating outside of their establishments.
- **Ask the shop class to design** and make benches for downtown.

WHILE YOU'RE AT IT:

- **Consider the accessibility** and make sure that people of all abilities can easily access and use the seating areas.
- **Think about the materials used,** while recycled materials can be a great option, make sure they are sturdy and safe for people to use.
- **Don't forget about maintenance** by adopting a bench, and keep it clean and inviting.
- **Consider adding planters or other decorative features or make** the seating areas more attractive.

FROM POSSIBILITIES TO REALITY | SAVE YOUR SMALL TOWN

BE IDEA FRIENDLY: GATHER YOUR CROWD, BUILD CONNECTIONS, TAKE SMALL STEPS

Where could you put accessible seating in your town?

_____

_____

_____

_____

_____

_____

_____

_____

_____

_____

_____

_____

CHECK IN:

What connections did you build? What worked and what didn't?
What small step will you/your crowd take and when?

_____

_____

_____

_____

_____

Tim Adams Art: https://www.timadamsartist.net/

Discover Textiles in Placemaking

TOWNS ARE DRESSING UP

You've heard the phrase 'placemaking' before. But just what is it? The Project for Public Places says "Placemaking is a participatory process for shaping public space that harnesses the ideas and assets of the people who use it."

This image is from the New Iberia Louisiana, population 27,473, Spanish Festival. Pictured is a crocheted ceiling at Church Alley in New Iberia. Their sister city in Spain inspired them.

WHAT ARE SOME WAYS TO USE QUILTS AS ART?

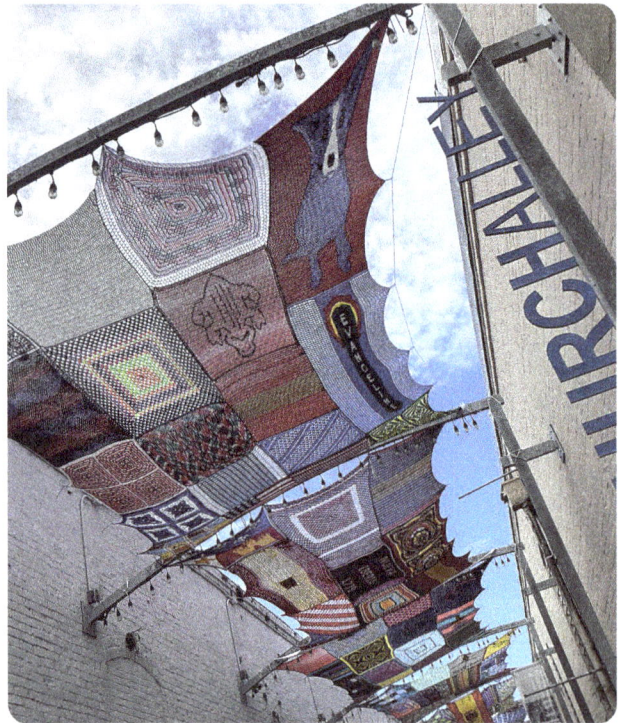

- Using quilt patterns as inspiration for murals or street art.
- Creating large-scale sculptures or installations using quilted fabric.
- Integrating quilts into public seating or benches.
- Use them as decorative pieces in parks and city halls.
- Displaying quilts as backdrops for outdoor concerts or other events.
- Hold quilt-making workshops to preserve your community's traditions.

BY COMBINING ART, CULTURE, AND COMMUNITY ENGAGEMENT, QUILTS CAN TRULY BECOME A BELOVED PART OF YOUR TOWN'S IDENTITY.

THEN THERE'S YARN BOMBING...

Bitrebels.com wrote about yarn bombing. I love these quilt-like pieces for chain link fences!

BE IDEA FRIENDLY: GATHER YOUR CROWD, BUILD CONNECTIONS, TAKE SMALL STEPS

My friend Jennifer Drinkwater is an artist in Iowa and has created a toolkit for yarn bombing – at no charge! Where could you yarn bomb in your area? https://whatsgoodproject.com/toolkits Where could you use traditional quilt patterns in a brand new way in your town?

YARN BOMB!

A Toolkit for Community Fiber Projects

YARN BOMB! A TOOLKIT FOR COMMUNITY FIBER PROJECTS

CHECK IN:

What connections did you build? What worked and what didn't?
What small step will you/your crowd take and when?

Bit Rebels yarn art: Bitrebels.com

Light Up Your Town

Success Story | IOWA CITY, IOWA | POPULATION 75,233

Leaders in Iowa City had a bright idea! Install additional lighting to make the downtown area more attractive to residents and visitors. Using different types of illumination makes it all more interesting. Select styles that can stay up around the year.

ADDITIONAL ILLUMINATION MAKES FOR A SAFER DOWNTOWN. PEOPLE WILL BE MORE APT TO VISIT IF THEY FEEL SECURE.

WHAT ARE SOME WAYS TO CREATE MORE ATMOSPHERE BY USING LIGHTS?

- **Install string lights** along main streets and pedestrian areas.
- **Use colored spotlights** to highlight architectural features of buildings.
- **Illuminate trees and foliage** with lights that either point into the trees or down on the sidewalks.
- **Hang lanterns** or other decorative fixtures in public spaces.
- **Create temporary light installations** for special events or holidays.

BONUS SECTION:

THERE'S A MOVEMENT CALLED DARK SKY LIGHTING. IT ALLOWS YOU TO LIGHT THE AREA, BUT ALSO BE ABLE TO SEE THE DARK SKY.

Explore: darksky.org

BE IDEA FRIENDLY: GATHER YOUR CROWD, BUILD CONNECTIONS, TAKE SMALL STEPS

What could you do to help your local businesses create more fun lighting downtown?
Find out if they're even interested. If so, there are a few ways to help! Research and write a grant. Help hang lights. Sponsor an installation. Just start with one business, remember – small steps!

CHECK IN:

What connections did you build? What worked and what didn't?
What small step will you/your crowd take and when?

Use Your Fences

Success Story | INDIANOLA, IOWA | POPULATION 16,069

Often it feels like construction projects take forever to complete. And if it is a city or county undertaking the job, the footprint to the town can be … extensive. Temporary fencing around a site is imperative, but let's face it, it's not attractive. Indianola, Iowa, experienced this in a big way when they renovated the courthouse square. For a while, there was a big hole in the middle of town surrounded by a chain link fence.

The county made the best of a messy situation by decorating the construction fencing with colorful banners that promote their county. They opened it up to the community for people to submit or sponsor their own banners. Since it's a multi-year project, they will continue to add more banners over time.

THEY'RE CALLING IT "WARREN COUNTY STRONG" TO REFLECT THE STRENGTH THAT THEIR COMMUNITIES ARE SHOWING DURING THIS TOUGH TIME!

Photo by Loren Ditzler

HOW CAN YOU USE FENCES TO MAKE YOUR COMMUNITY LOOK BETTER?

ADD DECORATIVE ELEMENTS SUCH AS:

- colorful slats
- climbing plants
- artistic murals
- banners that promote your town

BE IDEA FRIENDLY: GATHER YOUR CROWD, BUILD CONNECTIONS, TAKE SMALL STEPS

How could you use art to cover fences? Who are your gardeners who might plant flowers? What could your school art classes put together? What creative type will you talk to tomorrow to start the ball rolling?

_____

_____

_____

_____

_____

_____

_____

_____

_____

_____

CHECK IN:

What connections did you build? What worked and what didn't?
What small step will you/your crowd take and when?

_____

_____

_____

_____

_____

Warren County Strong: https://warrencountyhometownpride.wordpress.com/

Planters For All

Success Story | SOUTHAMPTON, ONTARIO | POPULATION 3,993

Almost every town has flower pots or planters downtown, and usually a few don't have anything growing in them. Start a campaign encouraging people, groups and businesses to take responsibility for maintaining a single planter or similar display. Challenge them to get creative, colorful … and consistent, so their work doesn't die for lack of water, fertilizer or weeding.

Jenny Amy told us: *"**We have Stealth Gardeners** in Southampton, Ontario, who come out and water potted plants that are sad and pull out weeds, and even sometimes spread mulch."* They work in the early morning or late evenings, so few people ever see them. They really are Stealth Gardeners.

OF COURSE, FLOWERS ARE GREAT, BUT THEY AREN'T THE ONLY GAME IN TOWN. HOW ABOUT SOME CHERRY TOMATO PLANTS, ORNAMENTAL PEPPERS, HERBS? MAKE IT CLEAR THAT PASSERS-BY ARE WELCOME TO TAKE A SAMPLE … JUST MARK THE PEPPERS WELL!

The Town of Lumby, British Columbia, population 2,000, plants herbs in pots on the utility poles downtown. Everyone is welcome to take some.

WHAT KIND OF COMMUNITY PROJECTS CAN YOU DO WITH FLOWER PLANTERS?

- Create a **community garden.**
- **Organize a flower planting event.**
- **Start a flower donation program** for hospitals or nursing homes.
- **Create a garden** for bees, butterflies, and other pollinators.
- **Start a "flower power" campaign** to encourage residents to plant flowers in their own yards or balconies.

Success Story | LINCOLN, ILLINOIS | POPULATION 13,084

Lincoln spearheaded a "Plant the Town Red" initiative. They sold thousands of red tulips to local residents to plant in their yards and along public thoroughfares. They've put over 40,000 tulips in the ground. They enjoy their splashes of red all over town each year.

THIS IS MY FAVORITE PARKING GARAGE! WHAT A GREAT IDEA TO PLANT FLOWERS IN FLOWER BOXES IN HUNTINGTON, WEST VIRGINIA, POPULATION 45,746

BE IDEA FRIENDLY: GATHER YOUR CROWD, BUILD CONNECTIONS, TAKE SMALL STEPS

Are there any areas in your town that could benefit from more flowers? Of course there are! Think of unusual places. And flowers don't need to be planted only by the Master Gardeners. Invite the community to plant flowers too. Who are your local gardening club members, or folks with fabulous flowers themselves?

CHECK IN:

What connections did you build? What worked and what didn't?
What small step will you/your crowd take and when?

Crafters Unite!

CRAFTERS CAN BE YOUR NEW ENTREPRENEURS

Art is economic development and giving our crafters a way to come together is important. You can boost creativity while building community with co-crafting events such as "crafternoons," or maker days. These are events where crafters/makers gather together and do their thing. Sometimes they are a one-off event, many times they happen on a regular schedule.

From tech enthusiasts to crafters, scientists to garage tinkerers, at these kinds of events, novices and experts of all ages come together to show what they've made and share what they're learning.

Your local library often is the place to find crafting events for kids and adults. Your senior center, churches, and gathering spaces are also places to look for crafters.

WHO IS A CRAFTER?

Potters, Quilters, Painters, Sculptors, Musicians, Cooks… artists of all kinds. Your makers also include all kinds of high tech and low tech, 3D printing and plasma cut metal signs but also blacksmiths. Search your town and your nearby town names on Etsy, Kickstarter and eBay.

WHY ARE CRAFTERS IMPORTANT TO ECONOMIC DEVELOPMENT? HOW CAN WE HELP THEM?

- They make special and unique things that machines can't copy. Many items are handmade.
- They bring different ideas and techniques.
- They bring antiques to the market and can help to keep traditional skills alive.
- Items made locally help keep money in town instead of going to some big nameless corporation.

TO HELP CRAFTERS WORK TOGETHER AND SELL THEIR PRODUCTS, WE CAN:

- Invite them to be pop-ups at events,
- Join online groups to find them.
- Give them places to sell their things.

WORKING TOGETHER CAN ALSO HELP THEM LEARN FROM EACH OTHER AND COME UP WITH NEW IDEAS. BY SUPPORTING CRAFTERS, WE CAN HELP THEM KEEP DOING WHAT THEY LOVE AND MAKE THE ECONOMY BETTER.

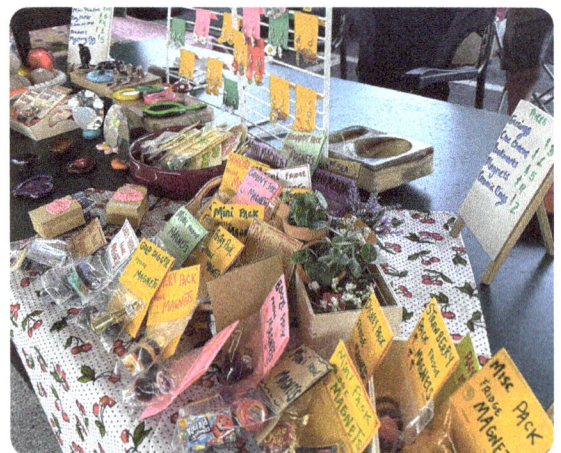

Jewelry, photo frames and refrigerator magnets are just a few crafting possibilities. Photo by Gregory Lakes

BE IDEA FRIENDLY: GATHER YOUR CROWD, BUILD CONNECTIONS, TAKE SMALL STEPS

Who are the crafters in your community? Time to make another list!

Ask on social media *'Who do you know who are Potters, Quilters, Painters, Sculptors, Musicians, Cooks, or artists of all kinds? That includes makers who are high tech and low tech, like 3D printing and plasma cut metal signs but also blacksmiths.'*

Kristin in Belle Fourche, South Dakota, posted on Facebook a request to list all the artists in town. There were lots of people added and many that she didn't know. You really don't know everything about everybody in small towns.

_____

_____

_____

_____

_____

_____

_____

_____

_____

CHECK IN:

What connections did you build? What worked and what didn't?
What small step will you/your crowd take and when?

_____

_____

_____

_____

There's a video for the *Idea Friendly Next Steps!* This is a $9 product from SaveYour.Town:
https://learnto.saveyour.town/idea-friendly-next-steps

Find Places To Beautify

Success Story | WEBSTER CITY, IOWA

Through a partnership with the University of Iowa, citizen volunteers worked together on enormous paint-by-number "snapshots" to dress up a second-story eyesore downtown.

THE ARTIST CREATED PAINT-BY-NUMBER PATTERNS ON EACH PLYWOOD "CANVAS." THE PANELS, CORRESPONDING COLOR CODE, AND PAINTS WERE MADE AVAILABLE AT THE FAIRGROUNDS FOR A COUPLE OF WEEKS. RESIDENTS WHO NEVER CONSIDERED THEMSELVES ARTISTS COULD PARTICIPATE BECAUSE OF THE EASE OF THE PAINT-BY-NUMBER APPROACH.

The images represent people, places and things important to Webster City's history. Lindsay Henderson was serving as community vitality director when she learned about the University of Iowa program and worked with the students and the locals to bring this project to life.

Photo of paintings by Michael Hansen

LEADERS IN GRAYSON, KENTUCKY DON'T SEE A BLANK WALL, BUT INSTEAD A BLANK CANVAS. WHAT A GREAT PLACE FOR A FUTURE MURAL! ALLEYS AND CROSSWALKS ALSO ARE GREAT SPACES FOR CHILDREN AND ADULTS TO GET CREATIVE, AND PROMOTE BUSINESSES AND TOURISM.

WHY CREATE A MORE PLEASING ATMOSPHERE IN YOUR TOWN?

Art, flowers, benches, and other beautification efforts provide several benefits, including:

• Creating **a sense of community pride and identity.**

• **Encouraging more foot traffic and increased business** for local shops and restaurants.

• Providing **a space for individuals to relax** and enjoy the outdoors.

• **Promoting physical activity** and exercise through walking and bike riding.

• **Attracting tourists** and visitors to the area.

DOES THIS REALLY MATTER?

Any time you are able to tell a positive story about your community, it matters. The artwork on the second- story building in Webster City created many opportunities to tell the story of the artwork, the community's involvement in making it happen, the outreach to youth and how it is used for tourism. Pictures on social media, newspaper articles, radio station interviews all came into play because of this action. It also helped uplift the community and the town members talked about the artwork to family out of town, to their youth who moved away, and to each other. That's promoting a small-town success story – and you can never have enough of that.

Promote your business with art

LAJUNTA, COLORADO | POPULATION 7,152

WHAT AN ATTRACTIVE WAY TO PROMOTE YOUR BUSINESS AND CREATE AFFORDABLE SIGNAGE!

ENID, OK | POPULATION 50,499

PAINTED THEIR CROSSWALKS

Photo by Enid Main Street

BE IDEA FRIENDLY: GATHER YOUR CROWD, BUILD CONNECTIONS, TAKE SMALL STEPS

I get asked, 'How do you pay for this?' Using paint? Check out the paint companies for grant possibilities. Keep America Beautiful has a community grant program, for example. Be sure you actually figure out what the costs are going to be! Often it is less than you can imagine. Write down ideas for how to pay for it.

_____

_____

_____

_____

_____

_____

_____

_____

_____

_____

_____

_____

CHECK IN:

What connections did you build? What worked and what didn't?
What small step will you/your crowd take and when?

_____

_____

_____

_____

_____

Dig Deeper

ART IS MORE THAN PRETTY THINGS

Rural food arts

FOOD IS ART.

We often don't consider food as art. Think about some of your favorite foods. Butter tarts, homemade tamales, chicken noodle soup -- these kinds of food tell a story of heritage, wellness and family. That's art. Farmers Markets bring people together sharing food they've grown and the food they've cooked.

A GOOD FARMERS MARKET IS A WORK OF ART. ENJOYED BY MANY, DOESN'T HAVE TO BE PERMANENT AND IT HELPS BUILD CONNECTIONS.

WHAT'S HAPPENING WITH GROCERY STORES AND WHAT CAN WE DO ABOUT IT?

We see many grocery stores folding in small towns, and the dollar stores moving in. There is a real lack of fresh fruits and vegetables, and meats you can cook (and not just heat up the box in the microwave).

When I was at a 3-Day Community Engagement visit in Siebert, Colorado, population 174, their grocery store had just closed. The city had access but didn't know how to make it a grocery again.

AFTER SHARING IDEAS, WE REALIZED THERE WERE PLENTY OF PEOPLE WHO GARDENED AND COULD SET UP IN THE OLD STORE ON THE WEEKENDS AND SELL THEIR GARDEN ITEMS.

Some people had flowers in their yards too, and they could sell cut flowers. **I encouraged them to start where they were with what they had.** Don't wait to fill it all up, just start. It could become an indoor farmers market pretty easily.

How to get started

IF YOU WANT TO START BUILDING YOUR FARMERS MARKET AS A VIABLE ALTERNATIVE WHEN YOU HAVE NO GROCERY STORE, THERE ARE OTHER THINGS YOU CAN DO.

- You can also visit other farmers markets and see what they are doing well.
- Have a conversation with the organizers.
- Reach out to your local extension office. They can be helpful and often know who's growing what in their gardens!
- It's also an opportunity to work with 4H kids in food production.

Success Story | ATHOL, MASSACHUSETTS | POPULATION 11,783

Mary wrote us a note about their farmers market.

"Our farmers market was dying. Vendors moved, organizers relocated, a shopping mall opened two miles away. We moved the market to a small space at one end of downtown and sales picked up. There was slower traffic, easier to walk to, higher density residential, and other attractions close by (hot dog cart, animal shelter flea markets, environmental center). Vendors started to return."

THEY DIDN'T GIVE UP, BUT THEY DID LOOK AT WHAT WAS NOT WORKING AND TRIED SOMETHING NEW. FAILURE IS NOT A BAD THING! IT'S AN OPPORTUNITY TO TRY SOMETHING ELSE.

A WORD OF EXPERIENCE:

We often hear as a rural challenge the people saying "We want things to be the way they were." This crowd often is pretty loud too. The vocal crowd is often in the minority, they just make the most noise. We call them the committee of negativity. Ignore them as best as possible! Starting your own small garden and sharing positive pictures and comments will go a long way. People like to see things in action first, and then decide if they should participate.

BE IDEA FRIENDLY: GATHER YOUR CROWD, BUILD CONNECTIONS, TAKE SMALL STEPS

There is a growing interest in foraging. Finding food in the forest and prairies that is considered wild. It's a topic that people are passionate about. Is there anyone in your area who could lead a workshop? Check with your County Conservation people. How could you add foraged foods to your farmers market?

_____

_____

_____

_____

_____

_____

_____

_____

_____

_____

CHECK IN:

What connections did you build? What worked and what didn't?
What small step will you/your crowd take and when?

_____

_____

_____

_____

_____

Links:

- Find other markets:
  https://www.ams.usda.gov/local-food-directories/farmersmarkets
- Learn more about foraging:
  https://smallbizsurvival.com/2021/08/rural-business-idea-forage-and-resell-free-fruit.html

Beta Readers

This book was not written all alone. The flow, structure, better stories, encouragement and some wisdom came from my Beta Readers. Thank you to these wonderful people!

JENN FARWELL	SVP OF PROGRAMMING	INNOVATION COLLECTIVE
LAURIE (BUNNY) BUNKER	DIRECTOR	BRONCS.ORG
STEVE FORTIER	ADMINISTRATOR OF RURAL ECONOMIC DEVELOPMENT, NH DEPT OF BUSINESS & ECONOMIC AFFAIRS
RUTH THOM	PEMBINA, NORTH DAKOTA
KIM LOZANO	EDITOR AND WRITING COACH	KIMLOZANO.COM
MELINDA (BURSON) MCGUIRE	COLLEGE INSTRUCTOR	MELMCGUIRE.COM
STEPHANIE OLSON	TAHSIS, BRITISH COLUMBIA, CANADA
LINDA SMUK	ITUNA, SASKATCHEWAN, CANADA
BRAD LINGAFELTER	MAYOR- HAVILAND, KANSAS
JOHN C. SHEPARD	AICP	VICE-CHAIR, APA SMALL TOWN & RURAL PLANNING (STAR) DIVISION
JACKIE KONEY	VICKSBURG, MICHIGAN
MAURY FORMAN	MAURYFORMAN.COM
JEN RISLEY	EDITOR, THE MAIN STREET JOURNAL
BETHANY FIFE	DIRECTOR OF COMMUNITY DEVELOPMENT, FROSTBURG, MARYLAND
RACHAEL MCKINNEY	COMMUNITY RELATIONS DIRECTOR, OBION COUNTY CHAMBER OF COMMERCE

Empty Buildings

We drive to work, we park the car, we work, we drive home.

Along the way we don't even notice what we see around us. Empty buildings, buildings that need their windows cleaned, buildings that need serious work – all of these are on our drive to work.

We think the nay-sayers might be right, this town is dying. It'll never get better. Why bother?

THE COMMITTEE OF NEGATIVITY IS NOT OUT TO HELP ANYONE! IGNORE THEM. THERE ARE THINGS YOU CAN DO.

Start by paying attention to your community. Notice the empty buildings, and the empty lots. – Think about how you as one person can battle the despair that has settled. **You can start with small steps by keeping your own surroundings happier looking.** Buy a plant and put it on the patio. Sweep your sidewalk. Wash your car more often. Smile more.

AND SHARE THIS SECTION WITH YOUR FRIENDS. THERE'S PLENTY TO BE DONE!

Have a Tour of Empty Buildings

14 EMPTY BUILDINGS DOWNTOWN

I went for an interview as Chamber Director in Webster City, Iowa, and counted 14 empty buildings downtown.

I KNEW MY NEW JOB WOULD BE TO FILL THEM.

I got the job. There was one big manufacturer and it had moved to Mexico two years before. That meant 2,000 people out of work; 2,000 people without the money to shop at the stores downtown. Their worst fears had materialized. And the town had the negative belief that this would never get better, our 'savior' company had left.

Businesses closed because they couldn't see a way forward. Building owners began to see how they could use their empty buildings as a tax write-off or fill it with storage. No one wanted to talk about all the empty buildings. No one. They were a sign of loss and who wants to focus on that?

I knew we couldn't continue to ignore those buildings. I believed that we could fill the buildings, and that RIGHT NOW there were people who wanted to fill them. I knew that we needed to show the buildings off, tell their stories, and dream about their futures. It would need to be a project filled with lots of people involved in small ways and very transparent. It would be a Tour of Empty Buildings.

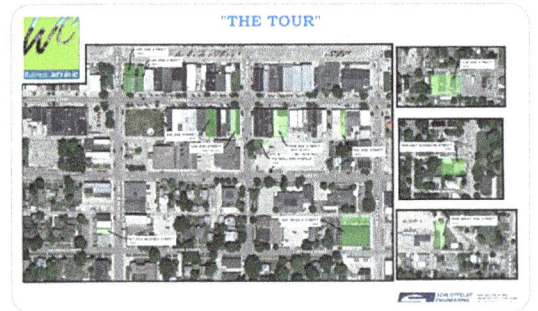

WE NEEDED TO STOP TALKING ABOUT 'IT USED TO BE THIS WAY' AND START TALKING ABOUT THE POSITIVE WAYS TO FILL THE BUILDINGS GOING FORWARD.

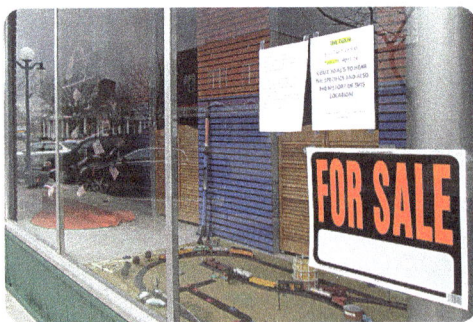

Results

The day of the tour came, and 44 people attended. We considered it a success. Several people talked about buying buildings and starting new businesses. At the wrap-up coffee gathering, everyone was excited.

But the small steps didn't stop there. During the tour, our chamber champions not only told the history of the building but shared their ideas about what could be in them in the future. It sparked conversations and ideas, and they continued to follow up with people they spoke to.

Some of our local business people shared the list of buildings with people they knew and encouraged them to move to a town 'that was moving forward.'

I wrote press releases from our chamber and sent them to other chambers, and economic developers and state contacts.

IN 18 MONTHS, 10 OF THE BUILDINGS WERE FILLED!

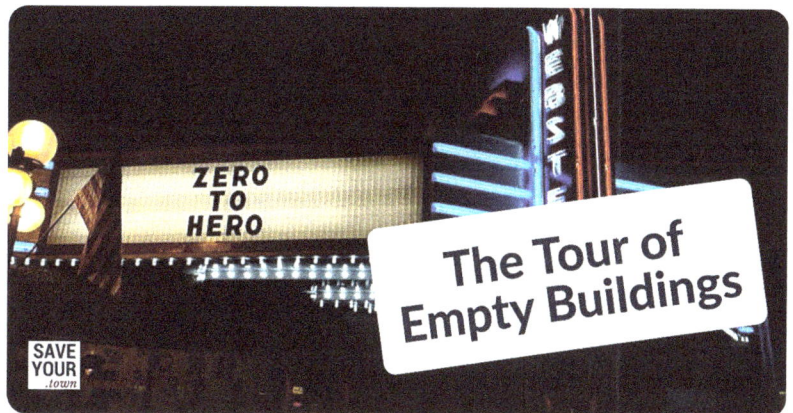

The Tour of Empty Buildings

WE'VE MADE THIS ONE EASY FOR YOU. LEARN HOW TO HOST YOUR OWN TOUR WITH THIS $100 TOOLKIT:

https://learnto.saveyour.town/tour-of-empty-buildings-toolkit

The Tour of Empty Buildings resulted in new businesses, filled buildings, changed how locals thought of their town and drew national attention. It also inspired other towns to show off their empty buildings as an asset.

IF YOU'VE HEARD THE IDEA AND NODDED, THINKING "WHAT A GREAT IDEA! WE COULD DO THAT HERE!" BUT YOU DIDN'T ACTUALLY GET IT DONE, THE TOUR KIT MAY BE JUST THE HELP YOU NEED.

It will help you go from "great idea!" to "I'm so glad we did it!"

You'll get four lessons, walking you through the whole process, step by step. You can save them for later or print them out if you like.

BE IDEA FRIENDLY: GATHER YOUR CROWD, BUILD CONNECTIONS, TAKE SMALL STEPS

Jane Priebe from Wahpeton, ND shared this note with us:

We recently held our first of three Tour of Empty Spaces. We realized that not all buildings were completely empty but that maybe had empty spaces within the structure that could be put to good use. We had about 30 people attend the self-guided tours although we had volunteers stationed at each location…11 of them. Afterwards we held a "Clink and Think" as a way to brainstorm what could go in there. Gathered up the post-it notes and now the local Young Professionals [who will be renaming themselves to be more inclusive] will run with the next two. Our office, Wahpeton Economic Development in the city of Wahpeton basically set up the first one with help from volunteers. We feel it was a success and got the chatter going! Our "listings" were on our city website. Thanks for the idea!

Start your own tour of empty buildings list!

CHECK IN:

What connections did you build? What worked and what didn't?
What small step will you/your crowd take and when?

Tour of Empty Buildings Toolkit. This is a $100 product from SaveYour.Town:

https://learnto.saveyour.town/tour-of-empty-buildings-toolkit

Make Empty Buildings More Appealing

Success Story | HOLLIS, OKLAHOMA | POPULATION 2,060

Nope, it is not a set from a Gary Cooper western; it is a banner inside of the building made to look like a barbershop. Even the barber pole wall is a printed banner hung inside an empty building. Betty Motley helped start Harmon County Forward, which is simply a group of people who are saving their town.

THEY SAW A NEED AND ADDRESSED IT WITH FUN AND CREATIVITY.

Photo by Betty Motley, Harmon County Forward

Success Story | COLUMBIANA, OHIO | POPULATION 6,713

The owner of this building didn't want to put in a window until he had a renter. He wanted to install a window specifically for the new tenant's needs. Makes sense, doesn't it? Yes, but the result was an unsightly boarded-up storefront.

A local artist was hired to paint this scene and worked on this painting during an outdoor festival downtown. Festival goers enjoyed his work and got to tour the building.

COLUMBIANA WAS VOTED BY AMERICA IN THE READER'S DIGEST CONTEST AS THE NICEST PLACE IN AMERICA, AFTER MY VISIT!

(Columbiana is the city mentioned in the Forward who furnished the kind words there.)

What are other ideas to make your windows more attractive?

- **Install colorful curtains or drapes** that complement the building's exterior.
- Use vinyl decals, window clings or stickers to **create a visually interesting design** on the windows.
- **Hang temporary artwork or posters** inside the windows to create a gallery-like effect.
- **Place potted plants or flowers on the windowsill** to add a touch of nature and color.
- **Use lighting to highlight the windows** and draw attention to the building, especially at night.
- If the building is located in a busy area, **use the windows to advertise upcoming events or promotions.**
- **Use the windows to display a video or animation.**
- **Highlight the history or architectural features** through the window displays.
- Finally, **partner with local artists or community groups to create rotating window** displays.

Success Story | TEKOA, WASHINGTON | POPULATION 807

Mayor Roy Schulz from Tekoa, shared this picture from one of their empty buildings. It's a simple idea to share photos of locals doing some great things!

BE IDEA FRIENDLY: GATHER YOUR CROWD, BUILD CONNECTIONS, TAKE SMALL STEPS

There are many great ideas above! I also like inviting your local service clubs to decorate one of your windows for a short period. When I sold luggage for a living, we partnered with the local art school and featured artwork alongside our luggage in the windows. It brought people to the store every month to look at the artwork … AND luggage! What are some ideas for windows in your downtown?

You don't know who Gary Cooper is? Don't feel bad, he's a real old cowboy. I looked for some other references to barbershops in the movies and found a cool site from a couple of barbers in Colorado. https://www.semionbarbershop.com/2014/05/10/barbershops-in-the-movies/ I love how they are using this information on their small business website! Great marketing, and an idea you can copy too!

CHECK IN:

What connections did you build? What worked and what didn't?
What small step will you/your crowd take and when?

Links:

• Columbiana is the Nicest Place in America:
  https://www.rd.com/article/columbiana-ohio-nicest-place-in-america/

• Harmon County Forward: https://www.facebook.com/HarmonCountyForward

Empty Lots

Success Story | PORTERDALE, GEORGIA | POPULATION 1,845

Porterdale, Georgia had a huge community center and gymnasium that was 12,000 square feet. It was built in 1939, and designed by Ellamae Ellis League. That's right, a woman designed the original building. Almost unheard of.

It burned down in 2005, and the cause of the fire was never found. It was located downtown and looked pretty awful. To completely rebuild the project would've cost in the $4 million range. That was not in the city budget!

So they put their heads together and came up with another idea. It became an adaptive reuse project, and the cost was under $1 million. Still a hefty sum; however, the community agreed to a 1% Special Purpose Local Option Sales Tax (SPLOST.)

It was stabilized in 2012 and completed in 2013. It's now an event space that has hosted concerts, food festivals, and weddings. For a town with only 1,281 people, it's now a huge asset instead of a huge eyesore.

Rural folks seldom give up. When local people put their heads together and come up with doable ideas, they help their towns to prosper, too.

SAME PLACE – WHAT A GREAT TRANSFORMATION!

Photos by Teri Haler

Small towns don't have to settle for business as usual. And entrepreneurship is the best way to support small towns.

WHEN LOCAL PEOPLE START THEIR OWN BUSINESSES AND PROSPER, THEY HELP THEIR TOWNS TO PROSPER, TOO. RURAL ENTREPRENEURS ARE EXPLORING NEW SHAPES, NEW LOCATIONS, AND NEW WAYS OF DOING BUSINESS.

Success Story | TIONESTA, PENNSYLVANIA | POPULATION 500

This empty lot used to have a business there in Tionesta, PA, The block-long building burnt down. The lot sat empty for 10 years.

UNTIL SOMEONE HAD AN IDEA. WHAT IF THEY TOOK GARDEN SHEDS, DRESSED THEM UP, AND PUT THEM ON THIS LOT?

Photo by Forest County Industrial Development Group

Photo by Forest County Industrial Development Group

THIS IS WHAT IT LOOKS LIKE TODAY!

Use inexpensive garden sheds to create a bunch of tiny business spaces.

It's a kind of business incubator. It would work in a roofless building just as well as an empty lot.

THEY REALLY ARE GARDEN SHEDS! THERE ARE 11 OF THEM SET IN A HORSESHOE DESIGN.

This is the Tionesta Market Village:

https://www.facebook.com/p/Market-Village-300-Block-Tionesta-PA-100063761522108/

Success Story | PASCAGOULA, MISSISSIPPI | POPULATION 21,640

Pascagoula, Mississippi had a big ol' dirty lot in town. After Hurricane Katrina, somebody had a great idea to use the leftover housing from FEMA to build out Anchor Square. Put a deck around it too.

They had green space in front and room for pop-ups and small vendors to try their ideas out.

Many of these small businesses have moved into stores, and downtown is now thriving! Now there is a developer converting these buildings into downtown living spaces. Things are seldom permanent, and that's okay!

WHAT ARE SOME IDEAS FOR USING AN EMPTY LOT FOR A BUSINESS?

- **A community garden** or a small park with benches and picnic tables.
- **A makeshift sports field** for soccer, volleyball, or basketball.
- **Outdoor movie screenings** or live music events.
- **A temporary art installation** or sculpture garden.
- **A pop-up market** or flea market for local vendors and artists.
- **A food truck festival** or a potluck party where people can share their favorite dishes and enjoy each other's company.
- **A mini-library or book exchange** where people can borrow or donate books.
- **A community mural or graffiti art project** where people can express themselves creatively.

Success Story | ALVA, OKLAHOMA | POPULATION 4,998

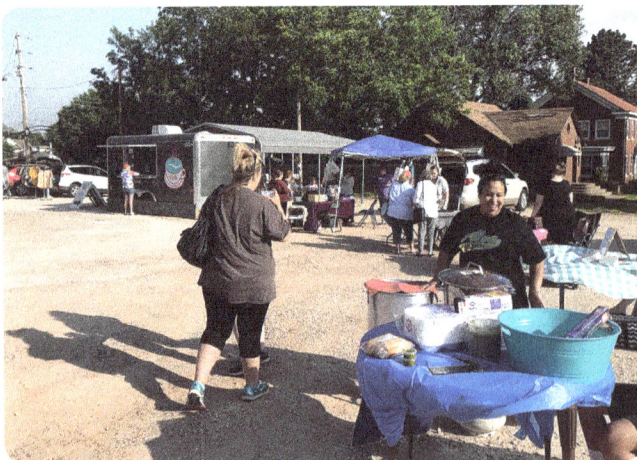

Alva residents found a use for this empty lot.

THEY STARTED THEIR OWN LITTLE PLACE TO GATHER AND EAT LOCAL FOODS!

Photo by Becky McCray

Success Story | ROCK SPRINGS, WYOMING | POPULATION 10,450

Rock Springs, Wyoming, took an empty lot and created a mini golf course. They also added a mural on the side of the building. Chad Banks from the Main Street/Urban Renewal group said *"The mini golf course opened in 2018. It was built using a grant and volunteers and has been really popular. It TRANSFORMED this corner that was just a lot full of weeds. We have re-done the holes once (last year) as the turf was wearing out . We have a little box where we ask folks to register (just to track numbers) and get about 300 registered each month in the summer. It's covered during the winter months. We have a large basket with putters and a small basket of balls, folks just take them on the honor system. We've never really had any problems."*

Photo by Chad Banks

WHERE COULD YOU DO THIS IN YOUR TOWN?

WHAT KIND OF RECREATIONAL IDEAS COULD BE TRIED IN AN EMPTY LOT?

- **A farmers market,**
- **A recreational area** such as a mini-golf course or outdoor entertainment space.
- **A green space** or park that can serve as a gathering place for the community. This can include amenities such as benches, picnic tables, and a playground for children.
- **A small popup business** that offers unique and locally made products. This can include selling handmade clothing and accessories, a specialty food shop, or a traveling bookstore.
- **Create a food truck** or mobile business park.

Create a Downtown Living Room

Success Story | LYONS, NEBRASKA | POPULATION 851

Make your empty lot comfier and home-like. Hold conversations there. In Lyons, Nebraska they had a temporary art/community project. The Center for Rural Affairs asked, "What makes your town special?" during "outdoor living room" events, where residents got comfortable in couches and chairs assembled along their town's main street. In an empty lot they placed a couch, a chair, a rug and a table and invited residents to come visit.

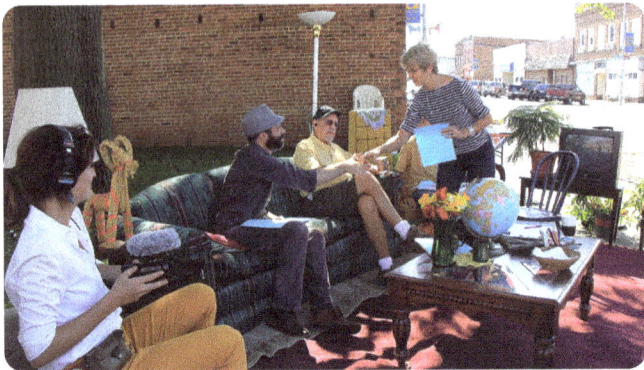

Photo by Center for Rural Affairs

YOU COULD DO THIS IN YOUR TOWN!

It could be a place where the mayor, or anyone can set up and invite people to come talk about any topic. It could also be in a roofless building, or an empty building.

WHAT ARE SOME IDEAS FOR CREATING A LIVING ROOM OUTSIDE IN AN EMPTY LOT?

Low-Budget ideas:

• Define the space with an **outdoor rug or pavers.**

• **Create seating areas** with outdoor furniture like chairs, sofas, and benches.

• **Add shade** with umbrellas, pergolas, or shade sails.

• **Incorporate lighting** for ambiance and functionality, such as string lights, lanterns, or solar-powered lights.

• **Include plants in containers (bring from home)** to add texture and color.

• **Make the space cozy** with outdoor pillows, throws, and blankets.

Over-the-top ideas:

• **Install a fire pit** or chiminea to provide warmth and a focal point.

• **Consider adding a water feature** like a fountain or pond for a calming effect.

This is just one idea to turn an empty lot into a gathering place. Let your imagination run a bit – what else could you put up in the empty lots? Do holiday pop-ups or a holiday market, or tie in with special events.

BE IDEA FRIENDLY: GATHER YOUR CROWD, BUILD CONNECTIONS, TAKE SMALL STEPS

These projects listed are great ideas, but what are smaller things you could do? Invite your local dance club to give performances, set up sprinklers for a quick splash pad, or ask the kids what kind of thing they want to do for one day. This brings attention to the people there, and the empty lot. It's a great way to begin filling your lots.

This is the Los Laureles Dancers from Perry, Iowa, population 8,008, performing at an art event in the park at Webster City, Iowa.

CHECK IN:

What connections did you build? What worked and what didn't?
What small step will you/your crowd take and when?

Links:

- Porterdale GA: https://www.facebook.com/TheVillageGemEventCenter/
- Market Village Tionesta PA: https://marketvillage-tionesta.com/index.html
- Pascagoula, MS Anchor Square:
  https://www.gulfcoast.org/listings/anchor-square-shopping-complex/3185/
  Lyons NE story https://www.cfra.org/

Dig Deeper

WHY ARE THE BUILDINGS EMPTY?

Empty building registries, fines and property maintenance codes

THERE ARE SOME CONSISTENT ANSWERS TO WHY BUILDING OWNERS KEEP THEIR BUILDINGS EMPTY, INCLUDING:

- **Lack of demand** for rental space.
- High maintenance or **renovation costs.**
- Difficulty finding **suitable tenants.**
- Using the building as a **tax write-off.**
- Using the building for **storage.**
- Simply **waiting for a more favorable real estate market.**
- **They can't afford** to do anything.

HERE ARE SOME OTHER POSSIBILITIES:

- **Lack of economic development:** If the town or surrounding area is experiencing a lack of economic growth, building owners may struggle to find tenants who can afford to rent the space. This can be especially true for commercial properties, where businesses may be hesitant to invest in a town that isn't growing.
- **Zoning regulations:** Depending on the town's zoning regulations, building owners may be limited in the types of tenants they can attract.
- **Aging population:** If the town has an aging population, there may be fewer people who are interested in renting space for businesses.

LET'S VISIT ABOUT WHAT YOU CAN DO ABOUT THAT.

Centerville, South Dakota, population 946, adopted a local vacant building ordinance that makes it costly to use empty spaces for cheap storage. Fees are charged for run-down, dilapidated properties. Dakota Resources has a Housing Toolkit you may want to use for reference in your area.

Fayetteville, North Carolina, population 208,873, targeted vacant commercial properties in their downtown, and started requiring inspection by the fire department every six months.

Empty building registries and fines

A register of empty buildings is a list of unoccupied or abandoned properties within a specific geographical area. It can be used to identify potential opportunities for real estate development or revitalization efforts.

HERE ARE SOME WAYS IN WHICH IT CAN BE USEFUL:

- **Identifying potential sites for new businesses or community services:** For example, they might use the information to target a new grocery store or healthcare facility to an underserved part of town.

- **Supporting revitalization efforts:** If a town is struggling economically, a register of empty buildings can be a key resource for revitalization efforts.

  By identifying which properties are available for redevelopment, community leaders can work with people **to bring new life to underutilized areas.**

- **Promoting historic preservation:** Many towns have historic buildings that are in danger of being lost due to neglect or lack of funding. By creating a register of these buildings, communities can work to preserve their history and character. People are often surprised at how many historic buildings they have in their towns. This is a good way to start talking about them – build a list of them.

Success Story | CALLENDER, IOWA | POPULATION 361
STANHOPE, IOWA | POPULATION 355

Callender and Stanhope have changed their city code and added a **Property Maintenance Code** for both the exterior and interior of buildings. I like it because it sets forth a detailed plan of action, a fine structure, and a no-nonsense "do this or we will take the building from you" attitude.

A property maintenance code is a set of regulations that govern the upkeep and safety of buildings.

- They can be used to **enforce maintenance standards** and ensure that buildings are safe and habitable.

- Property maintenance codes can help **prevent small maintenance issues from turning into major repairs.**
  WHICH CAN SAVE PROPERTY OWNERS MONEY IN THE LONG RUN.

- These codes often include **regulations around energy efficiency and sustainability** and can help reduce the carbon footprint of a community and promote environmental stewardship.

BE IDEA FRIENDLY: GATHER YOUR CROWD, BUILD CONNECTIONS, TAKE SMALL STEPS

There's a lot of information in this section. What can you do today to get started?

_____

_____

_____

_____

_____

_____

_____

_____

_____

_____

_____

_____

CHECK IN:

What connections did you build? What worked and what didn't?
What small step will you/your crowd take and when?

_____

_____

_____

_____

_____

Dakota Resources:

https://dakotaresources.org/wp-content/uploads/2023/03/Housing-Toolkit-shared-1.pdf

Try Targeted Incentives for Code Compliance

IT'S A KINDER WAY TO HELP THOSE BUILDING OWNERS

Instead of only having incentives for recruiting businesses, consider incentives to address the specific costs of compliance. Reach out to your city council members and elected officials. Your vote (or lack of) helped elect them and they have a responsibility to their constituents. Hold them to it. Attend the city council meetings and speak during the open public portion. You can also watch these meetings online.

WHAT ARE SOME INCENTIVES YOUR TOWN COULD BEGIN THAT ADDRESS THE COST OF CODE COMPLIANCE?

- Offer tax credits or exemptions for businesses or individuals who invest in code compliance measures.
- Provide grants or low-interest loans to help cover the costs of implementing necessary code updates.
- Streamline the permit application process to make it less burdensome for property owners and businesses.
- Offer recognition or awards to businesses and property owners who have gone above and beyond in meeting code compliance standards, to incentivize others to follow suit.
- Partner with professional associations and advocacy groups to promote code compliance and to offer resources and support to property owners and businesses.
- Rebates: Rebates are typically offered as a percentage of the cost of the energy-efficiency upgrades. For example, a city might offer a 20% rebate for the purchase and installation of energy-efficient windows.
- Waivers of fees: Cities can waive fees for permits and inspections for property owners who make energy-efficiency upgrades to their buildings. This can save property owners money and make the upgrades more affordable.

WHY DOES IT MATTER?

HERE'S WHAT'S POSSIBLE WHEN YOUR DOWNTOWN IS IN GOOD SHAPE.

- There's room for more new small businesses.
- These independent businesses support local families, community projects, keep profits in town and reduce sprawl.
- More jobs become available.
- Second-story housing gives people a choice in living arrangements.
- Healthy businesses in buildings assessed at full value generate taxes that give taxpayers a return on the public investment.
- Revitalization protects property values in surrounding residential neighborhoods.
- It stimulates the local economy.

And it's your home.

BE IDEA FRIENDLY: GATHER YOUR CROWD, BUILD CONNECTIONS, TAKE SMALL STEPS

This is an opportunity to sit down with your city council members or economic development folks and ask what the incentives are currently in your town. Begin the conversation over a cup of coffee, or with a couple of friends. DON'T ask at a city council meeting.

CHECK IN:

What connections did you build? What worked and what didn't?
What small step will you/your crowd take and when?

Empty Building Codes

Empty building codes are much different than a registry. The registry is your starting point: it's a list of the buildings that are empty. The empty buildings code is adopted by the city council and lays out in writing what happens if your building is empty.

WHY DON'T YOU HAVE AN EMPTY BUILDINGS CODE?

Are you sure your city doesn't have one? About ten years ago there was a vacant building ordinance included in the Webster City, Iowa code. It's still there today. Since it has not been used, many people thought there wasn't one!

THE BETTER QUESTION IS WHY ISN'T IT BEING ENFORCED?

One reason is there isn't an enforcement officer. Centerville, South Dakota hired someone to do code enforcement from the nearest big city. It was a savings to them – it was a contracted position and didn't require any benefits. The code officer was NOT known locally and the risk of giving people extra chances was not happening.

Success Story | WAYNOKA, OKLAHOMA | POPULATION 703
JEWEL, IOWA | POPULATION 1,187

Steal ideas from places like Waynoka, Oklahoma

It's a place where a group of citizens, the alumni club, got together and bought an empty building. They raised money with community events, had volunteer labor and accepted some donated materials that could be used to repair the building. They worked together to fix it, sell it, and buy another one. With that money, they bought another building. More work, more fundraising, even more work, and there's another building brought back into productive use. They keep doing this and fixing up their downtown, one building at a time.

Be a Jewel. Iowa, that is.

Rick Young, County supervisor said, "For example, the city of Jewel has spent $1 million in the last 30 years on their Main Street and very well done. Looks good."

But it started with just a group of people who invested in one empty building. And the town had plenty. Today you won't find an empty building in Jewel. But you will find several sheds, like garden sheds, that have been converted to a place where popups are in the summer, giving entrepreneurs a chance to try their ideas out.

Keep existing buildings up to code.

Pennsylvania has a toolkit for preventing blight, keeping properties up to code, and fighting long-term blight. Use the resources available already.

Review the report from Iowa's economic development director Debi Durham.

(The link is after the workbook page.) You'll learn about Tax Credits, Brownfield Funds, Catalyst Grants and Historic Preservation Tax Credits. This report is for Webster City, but it shares information you can use, too. It's good to go into conversations with some ideas to offer!

What does one empty building cost your community?

At the Brownfields West Virginia Annual Conference in 2022, Donovan Rypkema of Place Economics in Washington, DC, shared the calculations for the cost of one empty building. One building sitting empty for one year in a small-town commercial district will have the following impact on the community:

SOURCE OF LOSS	AMOUNT
ADVERTISING REVENUES TO LOCAL MEDIA	$3,500
BUSINESS PROFITS AND OWNER COMPENSATION	$24,750
EMPLOYEE PAYROLL	$16,250
FEES TO LOCAL ATTORNEYS AND OTHER PROFESSIONALS	$1,250
HOUSEHOLD INCOME GENERATED ELSEWHERE IN THE COMMUNITY	$18,900
LOAN DEMAND TO LOCAL BANKS FOR THE BUILDING	$51,000
LOAN DEMAND TO LOCAL BANKS FOR THE BUSINESS	$15,000
LOCAL DEPOSITS IN LOCAL BANKS	$5,100
PAYMENTS TO LOCAL UTILITY COMPANIES	$5,550
PROPERTY MANAGEMENT FEES	$750
PROPERTY TAX REVENUE TO THE LOCAL GOVERNMENT	$1,500
RENTS TO THE PROPERTY OWNER	$15,000
SALES	$250,000
SALES TAX REVENUE TO STATE AND LOCAL GOVERNMENT	$12,500

THE TOTAL IS **$406,050**

BONUS:

Follow Andrew Laddusaw on YouTube. He is cleaning up his town of Kittanning, Pennsylvania, population 3,923, and is offering solutions and stories of their work.

BE IDEA FRIENDLY: GATHER YOUR CROWD, BUILD CONNECTIONS, TAKE SMALL STEPS

Can you be a Waynoka, Oklahoma? Yes, you can. Start small. Watch a few videos on Andrew's channel. What ideas can you steal from them? What will be the first place you start?

_____

_____

_____

_____

_____

_____

_____

CHECK IN:

What connections did you build? What worked and what didn't?
What small step will you/your crowd take and when?

_____

_____

_____

Links:

- Building Code Webster City: https://library.municode.com/ia/webster_city/codes/code_of_ordinances?nodeId=COOR_CH10BUCO_ARTIVPUIMST_SS10-204--10-229RE

- Waynoka: https://smallbizsurvival.com/2018/03/small-town-neighbors-bought-vacant-buildings-brought-code-heres-happened-next.html

- Toolkit: https://housingalliancepa.org/wp-content/uploads/BlighttoBrightrevJune2016PrintFriendly.pdf

- DebiDurham: https://visitwebstercityiowa.com/wp-content/uploads/2024/01/DDurham_WebsterCity_Jan2024-1-1.pdf

- City Codes can be changed: https://buildingpossibility.com/articles/city-codes-can-be-changed/

- Dakota Resources Housing Toolkit: https://dakotaresources.org/wp-content/uploads/2023/03/Housing-Toolkit-shared-1.pdf

- Andrew Laddusaw: https://www.youtube.com/c/AndrewLaddusaw

Business

DOING BUSINESS IN A SMALL TOWN CAN BE A UNIQUE AND REWARDING EXPERIENCE. SMALL TOWNS OFFER A SENSE OF COMMUNITY, LESS COMPETITION, AND CLEAR BUSINESS NEEDS.

Whether it's opening a cozy coffee shop, starting a restaurant with a unique theme, or providing essential services like tutoring, event planning, or pet grooming, small towns offer a variety of opportunities to thrive.

Additionally, businesses that contribute to the overall quality of life, such as fitness centers, healthcare clinics, and childcare centers, can make a lasting impact in a small town.

MEET THE NEEDS OF THE LOCAL COMMUNITY AND START SMALL... TEST YOUR IDEA FIRST... SEE IF PEOPLE LIKE YOUR PRODUCT OR SERVICE. TRY IT LOCALLY AND TRY IT ONLINE, TOO.

Try an Incubator Project

Success Story | DOWNTOWN WEBSTER CITY | IOWA

I created the informal incubator project in Webster City, Iowa. Incubators are intended to help businesses try out their ideas, test the market and grow.

There was a building owner that had several buildings downtown that were empty. I approached them with the incubator project idea. I asked them to put their buildings in the program and offer three months free rent and reduced rent the rest of the year. The chamber agreed to help the businesses that went into those buildings with marketing, and the SBDC (Small Business Development Center) came in to help the business with creating a valuable business plan. Businesses could stay as long as they wanted the first year and would sign a lease the second year.

BENEFITS TO THE OWNER:

At least someone was paying for their utilities. Every building needs love, and this provided that. The business could leave at any time (this is a way to test out your business idea), or they could stay as long as they wanted!

DID IT WORK? YES.

First, there was an Italian restaurant. They lasted a year and had to move because the husband got a much better job. No worries, the Mexican grocery store across the street wanted to open their own restaurant in their store. They were saving money for a commercial hood. They tried the incubator space out. **They got to experiment with different recipes, hours, and servers. They tested their idea out and found out it was a good one.** Today, they have a restaurant open in their own space.

Photo by Deb Brown

How can you work with an empty building owner and entrepreneurs to let possible businesses try out their ideas in these buildings?

- **Ask the owner to participate!** Try free rent for a period, and then reduced rent for the rest of the year. Have entrepreneurs pay the utilities.
- **Market the space as a pop-up location** that can be utilized for short-term experimentation for your local entrepreneurs.
- **It can be more than one business in a space.** Which could result in more businesses in town!
- **Offer flexible lease terms and reduced rent** to incentivize businesses to use the space for testing their ideas.
- **Provide access to resources such as mentorship,** networking opportunities, and funding. This can help businesses grow and thrive. **Offer additional services** like marketing support or product development resources.

BE IDEA FRIENDLY: GATHER YOUR CROWD, BUILD CONNECTIONS, TAKE SMALL STEPS

- What are the empty buildings in your community that might be a great place to try an incubator project? **Make a list.**

- Who are the entrepreneurs in town who might want to try out their idea in a building? Maybe it is three or four folks who could share a space. Remember that list you made of the artists in town? **Ask them!**

- Get the word out there's a space for a new business with help for the new entrepreneur.

- Post it on social media and keep talking about it.

_____

_____

_____

_____

_____

_____

_____

_____

_____

_____

CHECK IN:

What connections did you build? What worked and what didn't?
What small step will you/your crowd take and when?

_____

_____

_____

_____

_____

Read the story of how Webster City came back from a hard blow, told by Square:

https://squareup.com/us/en/dreams/webster-city

Divide and Share a Building

Success Story | WASHINGTON, IOWA | POPULATION 7,277

Make a space that multiple businesses can divide and share. It can be a space carefully designed for compatible small retail shops, like the one Cathy Lloyd shared with us from Washington, Iowa. There was an old empty department store downtown. It had been empty for over 10 years. A group of women gathered and talked about ideas to fill it. The Village was born and consisted of individual entrepreneurs, artisans, crafters, and makers. They had spaces from the size of a small table to the size of the back wall.

In this picture the table, the wall, the yellow furniture,– they are all stores. It is a perfect way for a person going into business for themselves to try out their idea and test the market. It's a low investment and not thousands of dollars to buy a building, fix it up, purchase inventory, and hope people will come in and shop.

Photo by Sarah Grunewaldt

WHAT KIND OF BUSINESSES COULD WORK TOGETHER IN ONE BUILDING?

They can be **complementary to each other** such as a coffee shop and a bookstore; a gym and a health food store; or a salon and a boutique. Or they can be **totally opposite,** like a hardware store and craft brew pub that's a real place shared with us on the Survey of Rural Challenges. Handelbend in O'Neill, Nebraska, population 3,551, started a brewpub to sell their handcrafted mugs, added a coffee bar for the daytime hours and a flower shop moved in too! Keep in mind the potential benefits it can bring to the community.

SOME OF THE ADVANTAGES OF HAVING BUSINESSES IN THE SAME BUILDING INCLUDE

- **Convenience for customers:** Multiple businesses make it easier for customers to access the products and services they need.
- **Increased foot traffic:** When one business attracts customers, it also brings in more visitors to other businesses in the same building.
- **Cost savings:** Sharing a space with another business can help reduce rent and utilities.
- **Collaborative opportunities:** Businesses can work together to create joint promotions or events.

BE IDEA FRIENDLY: GATHER YOUR CROWD, BUILD CONNECTIONS, TAKE SMALL STEPS

- Have you made a list of entrepreneurs working from their home, garage or coworking space? Start there.
- Now invite those folks to get together to talk about creating a shared space. You'll begin to build connections by finding out who the owners are of some empty buildings that might work for a shared space location.
- Another small step could be visiting another town where there's more than one business in a location. Talk to them, ask how it's going, learn what works and what doesn't from them.
- What are some stores or offices that seem to have way more space than they need? What kind of "match-making" is possible? (Maybe a hair stylist has space for jewelry by a local youth).

CHECK IN:

What connections did you build? What worked and what didn't?
What small step will you/your crowd take and when?

What is the Village? https://www.thevillagewashingtonia.com/

Plan or Participate in a Pop-Up Event

Success Story | WEBSTER CITY, IOWA | ONE NIGHT EVENT

If more people are going to buy locally, that means we need to find ways to fill our empty buildings and entice shoppers to come downtown.

Karen A. tested her product and researched opportunities to set up a pop-up store in her community. A one-night holiday event in Webster City, Iowa, population 7,750, was perfect. Her pop-up was in a vacant building that was for sale. When the event finished, she had sold out of her handmade scarves, hats, and gloves. Karen also said the experience taught her that she really didn't want to do business full-time in a brick and mortar shop. Too heavy on the production end, she said.

IMAGINE HOW MUCH MONEY SHE MIGHT HAVE LOST FIGURING THAT OUT THE HARD WAY! INSTEAD, SHE'S BUILT RELATIONSHIPS WITH LOCAL RETAILERS WHO SELL HER CREATIONS FOR HER.

WHY ARE POP UP EVENTS SUCCESSFUL?

- They **create a sense of spontaneity and excitement** for people who are always looking for something new and unique.

- They can **help businesses to build stronger relationships** with their customers by offering them a personalized experience that is tailored to them.

- They can be **held in unconventional locations,** such as warehouses, rooftops, or even in a shipping container. This allows businesses to tap into new audiences and markets that they may not have been able to reach before.

- They can be a great **way for businesses to showcase their brand** and products in a more creative and interactive way.

EMPTY LOT POP UP IN MCKEE, KENTUCKY

Jackson County Creative Community was offered use of an empty lot in downtown McKee, Kentucky, population 797, owned by Kathy Spurlock. In addition to the pop-up art fair, there was also a car show in town. What a great idea to draw a larger and more diverse crowd!

Special thanks to Greg Lakes, tourism director for Jackson County, for photos from the pop-up.

HOW DO YOU FIND THESE POSSIBLE POPUP ENTREPRENEURS?

- Look at who offers things for sale on Facebook. Do you have a local buy/sell group on Facebook? You might find some entrepreneurs there.

- Don't forget the ecommerce sites like Etsy and Kickstarter. You can search by location on both Kickstarter and Etsy.

- Ask online! Kristen from Belle Fourche, SD asked on Facebook who the local artists were. She wanted to bring together local artists and started on social media. You may have already started a list of possible entrepreneurs, they make great popups!

BE IDEA FRIENDLY: GATHER YOUR CROWD, BUILD CONNECTIONS, TAKE SMALL STEPS

- **Remember that list of entrepreneurs you made earlier?** Go back and look at it. Who on that list might want to try out a pop up?

- **What kind of fun event could you create around pop ups?** It doesn't have to be a city wide event – it can be a block party in your neighborhood. Invite those entrepreneurs to set up at your block party. The church ladies might want to make brownies to sell. Your kids might draw chalk art on people's driveways for the party.

_____

_____

_____

_____

_____

_____

_____

_____

_____

_____

CHECK IN:

What connections did you build? What worked and what didn't?
What small step will you/your crowd take and when?

_____

_____

_____

_____

_____

Attracting Remote Workers

YOU HAVE WHAT THEY WANT

Remote workers are often young families, but they also include older workers ready for a slower pace of life!

Mainstreet.org says at the end of the day, the strength of this trend will be determined by how communities position themselves to leverage this growing interest in rural and small towns.

WHAT CAN YOU DO TO POSITION YOUR TOWN TO LEVERAGE THIS GROWING INTEREST IN RURAL AND SMALL TOWNS?

PROMOTE YOUR ASSETS.

Recreational opportunities are just one thing people are looking for.

There are things you take for granted in your small town – things that other people are looking for! The lake where you go fishing is an asset. The dirt trails the kids like to ride on is an asset. Sustainable ecotourism is a hot topic. Football, soccer, basketball, baseball, pickleball and tennis are just a few activities you might have in your town.

Infrastructure matters.

Do you have buildings that were built in the 1800's? What is unique about them? This makes them an asset. Is there free Wi-Fi in your downtown? That's an asset. How is the broadband in your area? Do you have any forms of transportation for people? The bus that takes seniors to doctor appointments, a local cab service, Uber drivers – those are all valuable assets too.

Food matters too.

Farmers markets, community gardens, and local grocery stores are just a few examples of what people want.

The arts.

People are looking for cultural opportunities to explore the arts. Are there art installations? That includes the neat signage that tells your town's story. Festivals that have artists involved, from someone who paints faces to gallery displays of local artists' work. What are some of the old skills still being taught? Hardanger, crocheting, cooking, and blacksmithing are just a few examples.

BE IDEA FRIENDLY: GATHER YOUR CROWD, BUILD CONNECTIONS, TAKE SMALL STEPS

This is important. Everyone should do this. **START A LIST OF WHAT IS GOOD IN YOUR TOWN.**

Ask others to contribute to it. **Keep building it. Every little thing counts.**

For example, you've got four-leaf clovers in your park. Or your Fourth of July parade has fire trucks and drivers throwing out beads (okay, okay, I do live in Mississippi and beads are a big deal here.) You just never know what one small thing will matter to someone.

SHARE THE LIST, OFTEN.

_____

_____

_____

_____

_____

_____

_____

_____

CHECK IN:

What connections did you build? What worked and what didn't?
What small step will you/your crowd take and when?

_____

_____

_____

_____

Becky and I made this video about Remote Work Ready. This is a $9 video from SaveYour.Town:

https://learnto.saveyour.town/zoom-towns-remote-work

Tourism as Economic Development

SMALL TOWNS ARE DIFFERENT

Tourism as economic development makes sense. Get people from outside of your community to come visit your natural resources, your events, and your community. Have them shop in town, eat at the restaurants, get gas in town, and stay overnight in your hotels, and that will stimulate your economy. We can all see that picture pretty clearly.

WHY DO PEOPLE COME TO YOUR TOWN?

Some of the things we don't always see are why people want to come to our towns. It's no big deal to us to go down to the small beach at the lake and enjoy swimming. Or drive out to the woods and fish by the creek. How about enjoying the dirt track races? Or park the car on the main street, and sit on the benches, and listen to live music on Thursdays.

WHAT ELSE CAN YOU DO IN A SMALL TOWN?

Look for ghosts at sunset in the old cemetery or make etchings on paper of the headstones. Learn the history of that family at the local library. We can just walk into the fire station and ask for a tour and be treated to a hands-on amazing try-on-the-uniform kind of tour! Many things we take for granted we assume others in our town know about, but that's not true.

ASK PEOPLE 'WHAT ARE THE FUN THINGS TO DO IN TOWN?' MAKE A LIST OF THEM AND SHARE THEM. KEEP ADDING TO THAT LIST.

WHAT CAN YOU DO AS A LOCAL?

This year as you plan your vacations, why not plan a few days spent in your town? Look at that list and add some of those activities to your staycation. Enjoy time with your family and friends and think about each day as an adventure. Post pictures on the socials, just like you do when you are on vacation. Hashtag it! #stayhome #staycationintown

Bringing more people to our community as visitors is a step towards economic development. Seeing what an area offers in the way of recreation and entertainment helps to get people thinking 'Maybe I could live in a community like this.'

LOOKING FOR THE POSITIVE POSSIBILITIES MAKES YOUR TOWN EVEN GREATER FOR VISITORS AND THE LOCALS!

BE IDEA FRIENDLY: GATHER YOUR CROWD, BUILD CONNECTIONS, TAKE SMALL STEPS

- **It's time for another list!** Remember, you don't make this list all by yourself! Begin by writing down three things to do in your area. Not the typical 'parks, trails, rivers' things. But things like teeter-totter in Park X. Or the waterfall on the river that only shows up in March.

- **Then hand your list to someone else.** Let them add to it, and pass it on. You can do this virtually or in person!

CHECK IN:

- What connections did you build?
- What worked and what didn't?
- What small step will you/your crowd take and when?

Promotion and Marketing

It's always Marketing.

AND IT SURE IS. WORKING ON SOLVING A CHALLENGE DOESN'T HAPPEN IN A VACUUM. YOU NEED TO SHARE YOUR STORY IN ORDER TO OVERCOME THE CHALLENGE. THAT'S MARKETING.

The old way of marketing was limited to print (flyers, signs and newspapers) T.V. and radio. It's called the old way because it doesn't work like it used to. Print media has gotten expensive and magazine and newspaper readerships have dropped significantly. Television ads are not seen as much, we are watching more streaming channels and don't see many ads on those. Not to mention, they are expensive. Radio has a certain client that listens, but if you aren't appealing to those clients your message is unheard.

THE NEW WAY IS REACHING OUT IN DIFFERENT WAYS. Social media, podcasts, and some direct marketing are just a few. It's important to like, follow and share the posts from local businesses. Learn effective methods for using social media, it helps! This chapter covers some ideas that are cost effective and work!

Make Selfie Stations

Success Story | VAN BUREN COUNTY, IOWA | POPULATION 7,256

It seems that social media has become a component of just about everyone's life. The only variable is how much one uses it. Sure, not everyone feels the need to photograph each meal in real time, but who doesn't like a good selfie, especially when traveling? Take advantage of the selfie impulse and provide a fun, attractive backdrop in a public spot in town, indoors or outdoors.

Fabric and wood are great materials for a semi-permanent backdrop. Make it portable so it can be moved from venue to venue. Just need something for a one-day event? Go for cardboard or colored chalk.

THIS WHIMSICAL SELFIE STATION IS MADE AVAILABLE AT THE ANNUAL VAN BUREN COUNTY SCENIC DRIVE FESTIVAL.

You'll find arts and crafts vendors, antique vendors, art shows, music, garage sales, kid's entertainment, parade, car and motorcycle show, food, and more activities throughout the Villages. **Trivia: It's the only county in Iowa with no stoplights.**

WHAT KIND OF PROJECTS CAN YOU CREATE WHERE PEOPLE CAN TAKE SELFIES IN YOUR COMMUNITY?

Host a "Selfie Day" event where people can come together to take selfies and participate in community-building activities. This could include games, contests, and other fun activities that encourage people to connect with each other and their community.

Create a community photo album where people can submit their favorite photos of the community, including selfies. This could be a physical album that is displayed in a public space, or an online album that is shared through social media or a community website.

Partner with local businesses and organizations to **create a community selfie challenge.** Participants would be given a list of locations or landmarks to visit and take selfies at, with prizes awarded for completing the challenge.

Develop a community-wide social media campaign that encourages people to share their favorite photos and stories about the community. And use hashtags that allow people to easily find and share content.

Invite your art classes to make a selfie station. Family members want to see what their kids are up to, and they will visit the station too!

BE IDEA FRIENDLY: GATHER YOUR CROWD, BUILD CONNECTIONS, TAKE SMALL STEPS

Here's an idea – why not ask everyone to make their own selfie stations? Then make a selfie station tour map. This could be a fun temporary project – nothing permanent needed to try the idea out! What are your ideas?

CHECK IN:

What connections did you build? What worked and what didn't?
What small step will you/your crowd take and when?

Hashtag, Great Idea!

Success Story | PAULDING, OHIO | POPULATION 3,546

Want people to use your hashtags? Post them! You'll be getting more people to help promote your community.

When I visited Paulding, Ohio, there was a big sign painted on the wall of an empty building. It was advertising a business that was no longer there. And the building owner lived in China! Before I left, we covered it by painting their favorite hashtag promoting the town. And no, we did not ask for permission! Lots of people honked and cheered when they drove by, including the county sheriff. This was a good way to make more locals aware of the My Paulding hashtag.

Photo by Deb Brown

WHAT KIND OF HASHTAG IDEAS CAN YOU USE AS ART IN PUBLIC PLACES?

- Use a hashtag that promotes a theme in your town #ArtInOurTown.
- Use a hashtag that is interesting #SmallTownCool.
- Use a hashtag for a contest or event #OurTownSelfies.

HERE ARE SOME ADDITIONAL POINTS TO KEEP IN MIND:

- Collaborate with local artists and organizations to **create a sense of community ownership** and involvement in the project.
- Consider the location of your art. Is it **accessible and visible to a diverse audience?** Does it fit in with the surrounding environment?
- Think about the message and themes of your art. Are they **inclusive and representative of the community?**
- Consider the materials and techniques used to create your art. Are they **sustainable and safe for the public** and environment?
- **Encourage people to share their own photos and experiences with art.**

BE IDEA FRIENDLY: GATHER YOUR CROWD, BUILD CONNECTIONS, TAKE SMALL STEPS

There are some small steps you can take. Create a list of hashtags and share it on social media. Ask for positive input – what do people like? Encourage them to post the hashtags (both digitally and physically) and submit pictures and comments.

CHECK IN:

What connections did you build? What worked and what didn't? What small step will you/your crowd take and when?

I knew I was going to really enjoy working with Deb when she told us from the moment she steps off that plane to the time she heads back home, she will be there with us to share resources and ideas to revitalize our small towns. Then we had a planning meeting where she was immediately a member of our team pushing us to think bigger while selecting options that were easy to implement. Don't wait another minute to revitalize your small town."

Julie Flyckt
Adams County, Washington Economic Development Director

Dig Deeper
SHOP LOCAL

ARE YOU TIRED OF IT YET?

In today's mature retail landscape, the classic "shop local" message has lost some of its luster. Customers have heard it all before, and businesses are struggling to find new ways to capture their attention.

BUT FEAR NOT – THERE ARE INNOVATIVE STRATEGIES THAT CAN BREATHE NEW LIFE INTO THE LOCAL SHOPPING MOVEMENT.

UNDERSTAND YOUR AUDIENCE'S MOTIVATIONS

The key to driving real change is understanding what truly motivates your customers and business owners. It's not enough to simply preach the virtues of supporting the local economy. We have to dig deeper and uncover their hidden desires.

- **Customers** want convenience, speed, and experiences. They'll shop local when it aligns with their personal interests and makes them feel virtuous.

- **Business owners** have heard the "shop local" message loud and clear, but many are stuck in their ways. They need to be enticed with opportunities that directly benefit them.

CREATE ENGAGING EXPERIENCES

TO OVERCOME THE INERTIA OF A "MATURE MARKET" FOR SHOP LOCAL, WE NEED TO MOVE BEYOND GENERIC AWARENESS CAMPAIGNS AND CREATE EXPERIENCES THAT ACTIVELY ENGAGE BOTH CUSTOMERS AND BUSINESSES.

If you want to mobilize your shoppers, try Cash Mobs

A "cash mob" is a group of regular people who decide to all support the same local business on the same day. Picture you and 25 friends all showing up to the hardware store at the same time, each with $25 you're going to spend there. Think how excited the people will be, how surprised the merchant will be and how much of a difference you'll make in their day's sales total.

HERE'S HOW YOU DO IT.

• Pick one business at a time: concentrate your results in one place.

• Pick wisely: choose a beloved business everyone will love to support, like the drug store where the pharmacist has been a pillar of the community and a friend of the family to everyone. Or choose one that will be fun. Luling Texas picked the liquor store!

• Set an amount to spend that is enough to matter, but not so much it seems like a lot to spend. $20 is a good starting point. Maybe in your town, $5 is right. Just experiment.

• Then get the word out. Go online, pick up the telephone, text your friends, do whatever will work to reach people in your town.

• The organizers of one of the first cash mobs said they measured success by having one newcomer: one person they didn't know personally, who showed up and participated. That meant they had reached beyond their initial circle of friends.

• Take lots of pictures and post them ALL OVER online. Post pics while you're there and invite others. Go live with video! Make a big deal of making a difference.

• Then pick another business and do it again. Maybe a month later, it all depends on your town and your people. Use your pics from the last time to drum up interest in the next event. Pick a hashtag and use the same one every time, like #CashMobLuling.

HERE'S WHY THIS WORKS, AND WHY IT MATTERS.

• Notice how this isn't OLD WAY: It's not a campaign. It's not decided by a few in isolation. It's not a big project that's closed to experimentation.

• Notice how it is Idea Friendly: You're gathering a crowd of people using your network. People can participate at whatever level works for them, whether they come and spend money or just click "share" online. They don't have to commit to serving all year long. They can join in one time, and skip the next. It builds attention and starts conversations even among people who didn't go. And it is so fun, it's an event worth making the effort to be part of.

• According to the Fogg Behavioral Model, this is a Trigger. People already have a basic motivation to shop locally, and they have the ability to spend $20…, they just need something to "Trigger" them into action. The cash mob says this is the time, and this is the place and then people take action.

• **That one temporary action helps them reinforce their belief in themselves as people who shop locally because it matters. Do it more than once, and you strengthen the habit.**

• You're building a sense of community around shopping in local stores, making more people aware of what's available in the shops, and you're giving merchants a boost. That makes them more willing to work with you on other projects in the future.

• Cash mobs went viral a few years ago, and now the buzz has died down. That doesn't mean they aren't still great fun and worth the effort to create!

If you want to get your merchants working together, consider the Shop Hopping model.

Instead of a boring committee meeting that no one wants to go to, try this model that makes the get-together so valuable that people actually want to attend.

HERE'S HOW YOU DO IT.

- Yolanda Almaguer told us about her local group called Shop Hopping Around Brownsville. A group of people who have businesses decided to get together once a month at each others' businesses. The get-togethers only last an hour. Everyone gets to see what other businesses are doing, ask questions, get advice and look around.

- They might invite one person to share maybe a quick five minute talk about a practical topic or an upcoming chance to work together, but no more than that!

THE GOAL IS TO KEEP THESE FUN, LIGHT AND NOT AT ALL LIKE A COMMITTEE MEETING.

HERE'S WHY THIS WORKS, AND WHY IT MATTERS.

- In the old way you would never share anything about how things work in your business. In the Idea Friendly way business people want other business people to succeed. Sharing ideas helps each other out.

- When you start this kind of small project, there may only be a few people who participate. That's okay. They will talk about what happened, how cool it was and why they'll go to the next one.

THESE NEW BEHAVIORS FROM A FEW ENCOURAGE OTHERS TO ADAPT THEM AS NEW HABITS AS WELL.

- **We love this Idea Friendly way of business people learning about each other and learning about a few ideas they can try. It's gathering your crowd of business owners and networking with each other to learn the small steps some are taking.**

Another idea to get merchants to start working together is to start a simple gathering to share ideas

HERE'S HOW YOU DO IT.

- This doesn't really have a name, because it's just something we started doing in Hampton, Iowa. Someone said, "Let's go out to Judy's winery and talk about how we might work together." It was a loose gathering of local business people with no real set agenda.

- The business people were excited to participate in this "non-event", because it allowed them down-time to talk about partnerships that might work. There was no pressure to join in.

- We chose a time after the stores were closed. Judy from the winery had treats and wine for everyone. It was a very comfortable setting with cozy chairs. We talked about how customers weren't shopping in town. We also drank wine and told stories. **The focus was not on 'those awful locals who don't shop with us' but was on 'how can we partner together?"**

- We started talking about ways we could partner together to make some experiences for our customers – and bring folks into our businesses. **No idea was too small and all ideas were good enough to at least try.**

  - The other Judy, the one from Cornerstone Cottage, was opening a new children's store. Kim from the library put up flyers for the new store and shared some of the books that Judy would be carrying. Judy in turn shared information about the library's programming.

  - At the time I was doing marketing for businesses and also working for the Chamber in communications. I offered to take some pictures in their stores and share them on Facebook and tag them. They would share those posts and comment as well.

  - The local coffee shop invited local entrepreneurs to come set up. One of the other business owners first suggested it, and she liked the idea. She found that people were excited to showcase their handcrafted items, and they brought in more customers too!

HERE'S WHY THIS WORKS, AND WHY IT MATTERS.

- **It didn't matter if any of the ideas failed.** This was an opportunity to try ideas out, adjust if needed, and give it up if it just couldn't work. No shame involved. The Old Way would've involved giant projects and no small steps. There would be no room for failure.

- The emphasis was not on what the chamber could do for them. It was about taking small steps among themselves and having fun doing it. They found that they were a network for the community and each other.

- **The business owners found that working together made them stronger and they provided real value to the community for their shopping needs.** Their small steps and temporary behaviors led to locals interested in what they were doing, and created more permanent shopping habits. Now people knew to start with the merchants when they were looking for gifts, or coffee, or fun.

Try "one product" campaigns: One way of cutting through the clutter of a mature market is by targeting your message.

HERE'S HOW YOU DO IT.

• In Franklin County, Iowa, the Chamber started a **'buy one product local'** campaign. They chose toilet paper as the one product because we all need some! And because it sharpened the message.

• They found out how much money it could mean if everyone just bought their toilet paper in local stores. It was $1.9 million, enough to really get people's attention.

• The chamber did a complete year-long campaign, using all the tools you can think of to get the word out, offline and online. They did posters and radio and tv and made a special website.

• The committee made toilet paper displays that they took to every local event and fair and festival.

• The merchants got on board. They didn't just do signs, lots of them did creative displays. Imagine how much fun you can have creating a toilet-paper themed display!

THE LOCALS HAD A GREAT TIME VISITING STORES TO SEE ALL THE CRAZY DISPLAYS.

HERE'S WHY THIS WORKS, AND WHY IT MATTERS.

• The goal was to showcase the places to shop in the county, and to get people to think. Once people walked in the door to get toilet paper, you know they ended up buying other things – and even finding out about things they didn't know were available in town!

• It really worked because they didn't say "buy EVERYTHING locally" which is impossible-sounding. It was just "buy ONE PRODUCT locally" which is totally do-able. In Fogg Behavioral Model terms, this cuts down the size of the action, so people know they have the ability to act.

• While the campaign was going on, everyone in town was talking about toilet paper!

THEY WERE REDEFINING THEMSELVES AS PEOPLE WHO SUPPORTED THEIR TOWN BECAUSE THEY BOUGHT THEIR TOILET PAPER LOCALLY.

"We have more than you know" campaigns

This is more like a traditional average Shop Local campaign, so it might be easier to get a board to agree to it.

THE GOOD NEWS IS THAT THE MESSAGE IS MORE HELPFUL THAN PREACHY. HERE'S HOW YOU DO IT.

Imagine going around to local businesses, finding something you didn't know they had, and posting photos of that online. If you didn't know they have it, others don't know either! You can start this project with just you! You can go take pictures and post them.

EXAMPLES

- Becky did this for Shop Small Saturday in her town. And she found something surprising in every single store she visited.

- The Waynoka, Oklahoma, Chamber of Commerce has "Where is it in Waynoka Wednesdays." They post a few photos of a local business, featuring things people might not know they have. For the grocery store, they posted pictures of the gift wrap, the tools, markers and pens, auto supplies like oil… you get the idea!

HERE'S WHY THIS WORKS, AND WHY IT MATTERS.

- You're helping people find out about things they didn't know they could buy or support in town. You're sharing information in a non-threatening way and it encourages people to take a temporary action and go buy that product locally.

- It's so easy to do! Just simple online posts, photos and a few words, or a quick live video.

- It's an Idea Friendly way to do something on your own that invites others to join the crowd. You invite others to participate if they wish too. Networking pulls in the businesses and they can point out things in their businesses that you didn't know about. You'll take small steps by simply taking pictures and sharing them.

- A bonus is that you'll build connections with local store owners and other partners. Community happens when people talk to each other, even when they're there to take photos to post online.

Today customers can go anywhere and shop, including online. Keep this question top of mind:

WHAT KIND OF EXPERIENCE ARE YOUR BUSINESSES GIVING PEOPLE IN EXCHANGE FOR THEM AT LEAST BEGINNING THEIR SHOPPING AT HOME?

BE IDEA FRIENDLY: GATHER YOUR CROWD, BUILD CONNECTIONS, TAKE SMALL STEPS

Who can you meet with to brainstorm about what the new Shop Local might look like in your community? Take one of the examples, and create a flurry of associated names, products, and possible photo posts. Whose store will you go into and strike up a conversation about those ideas?

CHECK IN:

- What connections did you build?
- What worked and what didn't?
- What small step will you/your crowd take and when?

Toilet paper article in Dodge City:

https://www.dkcoks.gov/DocumentCenter/View/2787/2013-January

Funding

Funding is often the first thing folks want to talk about.

"HOW CAN WE AFFORD THIS" OR
"HOW CAN WE PAY FOR THIS?"

If you're using the Idea Friendly Method, you start with small steps that don't take a huge grant to pay for them!

Rural communities are very good at figuring out how to come together to help a project, save a building, put out a fire or do something for the kids. Take lessons from those experiences.

The successful projects have three things in common

THEY HAVE A NEED.

THEY HAVE A STORY THAT SOLVES THE NEED.

THEY KEEP TELLING THE STORY.

HERE'S AN EXAMPLE FROM WEBSTER CITY, IOWA,

that shares those three things.

1 — Our movie theater closed down.

2 — We came together and figured out what we needed to do to open the theater again. We raised money in small ways: donations as small as $5, sold the theater seats for $300, and Alumni clubs donated funds. There were people who volunteered to clean out the theater, and bought old movie posters and shared about it everywhere.

3 — We kept telling the story and got attention from the media around the United States and from the company SquareUp, which provides ways for people to accept money for payment. SquareUp also wants to tell the stories of communities who are doing helpful things. They came and filmed a movie about our factory closing and how we saved the movie theater.

FIND YOUR STORY THAT TALKS ABOUT YOUR CHALLENGE IN A WAY THAT PEOPLE CAN RELATE TO. AND THAT MAKES THEM FEEL THEY WANT TO BE PART OF THE SOLUTION.

KEEP TELLING YOUR STORY!

Fundraisers Everyone Wants To Participate In

PUT THE 'FUN' BACK IN FUNDRAISER

Do you have to do fundraising? Well, here's an event idea. It's a "no pancake" pancake breakfast. Many local service organizations ALWAYS make the pancakes at their annual fundraiser. They are starting to get old. And tired. So instead, sell tickets at $5 apiece. You buy your ticket, and on the day of the event you make your own breakfast and post pictures on your Facebook page! Not only does everyone have fun, but the old pancake makers are thrilled with the event, and they'll make more money than when they actually made pancakes.

WHAT ARE SOME EXCITING FUNDRAISING IDEAS?

• Partner with a local restaurant or brewery to **host a charity dinner or beer tasting event.**

• Organize **a scavenger hunt or treasure hunt** around town.

• Host **a movie night in the park or a drive-in movie** event.

• Hold a charity game tournament, such as a **poker or chess tournament.**

• Organize **a talent competition,** such as a singing or dancing contest.

• Partner with a local gym or fitness studio to **host a charity fitness class or bootcamp.**

• **Trivia nights** are big fun! Partner with a local bar or restaurant.

• **Flock of Flamingos.** You've probably seen this idea already, and it's a good one. A couple of additions to the process to make it more enjoyable. Make the amount to have them moved to another yard as a donation. Don't force people to pay. Offer flamingo insurance – you can pay to NOT be flocked!

• Bunny Bunker told us, "I like the charity poker tournament idea! I'm having the first fundraising event for my new rodeo horse rescue on May 4, we're calling it **Bronco de Mayo** and it's gonna be a big Western par-tay, including a 50/50 raffle and a horse shoe tournament."

• Our Junior Rodeo association used to hold a **poker night** as a fundraiser at the state finals. All kids were required to secure donations to be auctioned off at the end of the night with the "poker money" If you didn't have enough "poker money" you could use cash. This event raised $30,000 and more. (That was 20 years ago. Now they raise mega bucks!)

When I was with the group trying to save the local theater, we needed ways to raise money besides the usual bake sales and begging.

Alumni clubs are kind of a big deal in the town, so we decided to sell the seats at $300 a pop to lots of individuals, nonprofits, alumni clubs, and businesses. The local newspaper posted photos of everyone who bought a seat! It was a substantial chunk of funds raised.

DON'T FORGET YOUR ALUMNI!

Photo by Deb Brown

RECENTLY, THE CITY OF COLUMBIANA WAS LUCKY ENOUGH TO HOST DEB BROWN FOR AN EMBEDDED COMMUNITY EXPERIENCE. SHE MET WITH MANY INDIVIDUAL BUSINESS OWNERS AND MEMBERS OF OUR COMMUNITY, WHICH ALLOWED HER TO GATHER DATA TO PUT INTO A FINAL WRAP UP.

FROM THE MOMENT SHE ARRIVED, TO THE MOMENT SHE LEFT, SHE WAS WORKING VERY HARD SO SHE COULD PROVIDE IDEAS THAT WE CAN IMPLEMENT RIGHT AWAY. SHE HAS AN UNCANNY ABILITY TO TALK TO ANYONE, MAKING THEM FEEL COMFORTABLE ENOUGH TO OPEN UP TO HER.

I WOULD HIGHLY RECOMMEND ANY COMMUNITY INTERESTED IN IMPROVING THEIR FUTURE TO INVITE DEB BROWN TO VISIT THEIR TOWN. HER VISIT WAS DEFINITELY A HIGHLIGHT OF MY 21 YEARS WORKING IN SMALL GOVERNMENT."
LANCE WILLARD, CITY MANAGER

I WOULD HIGHLY RECOMMEND ANY COMMUNITY INTEREST IN IMPROVING THEIR FUTURE TO INVITE DEB BROWN TO VISIT THEIR TOWN.

BE IDEA FRIENDLY: GATHER YOUR CROWD, BUILD CONNECTIONS, TAKE SMALL STEPS

"Dancing with the Stars" has been very popular in several small towns, and a big money raiser. Pie auctions are fun too. What other ways could you enjoy fundraising?

CHECK IN:

What connections did you build? What worked and what didn't?
What small step will you/your crowd take and when?

Junior Rodeo story: https://borgenproject.org/non-event-fundraiser/

Old Paint

Success Story | PAINT THE STREET PROJECT

In Watertown, there was an empty space in a coffee shop waiting to be filled with another business. The coffee shop used the wall in the space to feature works by a local photographer. Many communities provide residents with a way to dispose of unwanted items that don't belong in a landfill and are not accepted through the municipal recycling program. Everything from furniture to motor oil to tires to mountains of batteries from TV remotes and other gadgets are accepted. In Webster City, Iowa, the mayor had a special interest in paint.

As residents dropped off those open cans left over from countless home improvement projects, the mayor snagged the ones that still had life left in them. Those dribs and drabs of color were used in the Paint the Street Project. Participating businesses paid $50 to paint a design on a selected street in one section. It was all about sprucing up the community. The funds raised went to support another arts event. Each year they paint over the designs with white paint and start again. And the mayor was able to kick this off by getting that usable paint at no cost.

WHAT KIND OF PROJECTS CAN YOU CREATE AROUND YOUR COMMUNITY USING OLD PAINT?

- **Repaint park benches.**

- **Create murals or street art.**

- **Paint fences.**

- **Beautify community gardens.**

- **Host a community paint day** where neighbors and volunteers can come together to paint a community space or building.

- **Create a public art project** where members of the community can contribute to a larger piece of artwork.

- **Create signage for community events** or to spruce up the exterior of local businesses.

- **Start a neighborhood beautification project** where residents can work together to paint and improve their homes or apartment buildings.

BE IDEA FRIENDLY: GATHER YOUR CROWD, BUILD CONNECTIONS, TAKE SMALL STEPS

What are some frugal ways you can think of to raise not just funds but donations for your special events?

CHECK IN:

What connections did you build? What worked and what didn't?
What small step will you/your crowd take and when?

Paint the Street Project: https://fb.watch/koOUb9v4uP/

Fill the Empty Walls

Success Story | WATERTOWN, MINNESOTA | POPULATION 4,842

This was an empty space inside a coffee shop. They used the wall to feature works by a local photographer.

You could do this in any business with a blank wall. It doesn't have to be retail. It could be a service business, too. Your local insurance office might need sprucing up with some local art.

Check with your student art groups too. Could you display their work with contact info?

SOME OTHER CREATIVE WAYS TO USE A BLANK WALL FOR FUNDRAISING INCLUDE:

1 — **Silent Auction Wall:** You can turn a blank wall into a source of fundraising revenue by using it for a silent auction. This can be a great way to engage possible event attendees and raise funds.

2 — **Interactive Donor Wall:** Incorporate interactive elements such as art displays into a donor wall to inspire donations. This could involve any form of art installation, creating an engaging and visually appealing way to attract donors and support fundraising efforts.

3 — **Community Envelope Wall:** Set up an envelope fundraiser on a community wall, where individuals can donate by taking an envelope and contributing the amount specified on the envelope. This can be a simple yet effective way to gather unrestricted funds and engage the community in fundraising.

CAN YOU PROMOTE ANOTHER BUSINESS BY USING AN EMPTY WALL IN YOUR BUSINESS?

- **Display advertisements or posters** for other businesses in exchange for a fee or a mutual promotion agreement.
- Offer to **sell their products or services** in your store or office.
- **Collaborate on a joint event** or promotion.
- **Share each other's social media posts** or create co-branded content.
- **Offer a referral program.** If you know your customers often are in need of services that another business provides, you could offer a referral bonus for each customer they send your way.

BE IDEA FRIENDLY: GATHER YOUR CROWD, BUILD CONNECTIONS, TAKE SMALL STEPS

CHECK IN:

What connections did you build? What worked and what didn't?
What small step will you/your crowd take and when?

Idea friendly officials and boards video. This is a $9 video from SaveYour.Town:
https://learnto.saveyour.town/small-town-officials-and-boards-idea-friendly

Consider a Transient Occupancy Tax

A VISITORS-ONLY TAX

Not many people want to think about taxes. In this case, the taxes are paid by visitors to your community! Let's consider the benefits of a "heads on beds," tourism or accommodation tax. Only lodgers at a community's hotels/motels pay this tax. Tim Truett, state representative for Jackson County, Kentucky attended a gathering we had when I was there for a 3 Day Community Engagement. He had not realized that people were interested in this idea, and added it to the next county meeting to be discussed. Reaching out to your elected representatives with suggestions helps.

Tim Truett represents the 89th Legislative District in Kentucky's General Assembly.

KENTUCKY ALLOWS COUNTIES TO CHARGE 3% TO LODGERS. FOR EXAMPLE:

If we average the 58 establishments in Jackson County and they book 15 rooms a month – that's 2,610 rooms. If each room is $100 a night, that will bring in almost $8,000 a month in tax revenue for the county. Now, I'm not the best at math, and I don't have a clue what each region will bring in, but you get the idea!

The transient occupancy tax generates revenue for the local economy, including funding for tourism promotion, infrastructure improvements, and public services. Each state (or province) has its own tax requirements, so it's important to get the details right.

When I was visiting the area, I stayed at Clover Bottom Bed & Breakfast in McKee. My hosts were Readith (center) and Greg Lake.
https://www.cloverbottombandb.com/

BE IDEA FRIENDLY: GATHER YOUR CROWD, BUILD CONNECTIONS, TAKE SMALL STEPS

Do some research. What are the options for your community? What other communities around you might be using this tax? Take a road trip with some friends and visit these folks. Understand that it is a tax to visitors, not to residents.

CHECK IN:

What connections did you build? What worked and what didn't?
What small step will you/your crowd take and when?

State Lodging Tax Requirements:

https://www.avalara.com/mylodgetax/en/resources/state-lodging-tax-requirements.html

Find Your People

Every town has people and assets to build upon.

IT'S ALL ABOUT EVERYONE BEING ABLE
TO PARTICIPATE IN SOME SMALL
BUT MEANINGFUL WAY.

Find your people. Leaders, volunteers, small steppers, and kids.

Your town

is a reflection of the people who live there.

WHAT ARE YOU DOING TO CREATE THE KIND
OF PLACE PEOPLE CAN CALL HOME?

Create More Community Leaders

LOOK EVERYWHERE FOR NEW LEADERS

Creating reasons for locals to stay is vital. They are the backbone of your community.

One way to find reasons for locals to stay is to let them lead. Of course, I encourage everyone to run for office if you don't like what's going on, but leadership comes in other forms. Not everyone will want to run for office, but everyone has ideas! And you've also got people you know who want to help you bring ideas to reality.

HOW DO YOU CREATE MORE COMMUNITY LEADERS?

IT'S IMPORTANT TO REMEMBER THAT LEADERSHIP DEVELOPMENT IS AN ONGOING PROCESS THAT REQUIRES COMMITMENT AND COLLABORATION FROM ALL MEMBERS OF THE COMMUNITY.

Good leaders must be open-minded.
Openness allows everyone in the town to have a say in local affairs and projects. Involving more people in decision-making helps your town find what the community really wants and needs and gets more people to volunteer time and money.

Be inclusive.
There's room for leaders from all walks of life and that represent the entire community. The towns that are led by a set group of people that accept no input are not thriving. The New Ways involve input from many people working together on innovative ideas and building connections to grow your community.

Engage young people.
Listen to your youth. Ask them what they want. Then let them try their ideas out. Put them on your city council as a non-voting member, as we were talking about earlier. Hear their input.

Partner Up.
Ask your seniors to partner with your students to participate in a project. Capturing oral history is a good project to start with. The young people will learn a lesson in leadership from these histories!

Find the people.
We tend to hang out with people we know. How can you meet new people in town? Attend events where parents are likely to be – dance contests, soccer games, and the pool come to mind. How about older people? Visit the coffee shops and join in the conversation. Go to the nursing homes and have lunch with the folks there. Stop by the historical museum and talk to the volunteers.

Akron, Iowa, hosted a **Plant Your Flag Party,** led by the mayor. Everyone was invited to come with their ideas for their town. No discussion was about what they didn't have. Instead, they talked about what they wanted. And they got into action right away. The folks that showed up with ideas were all leaders. Not necessarily known as leaders in town, but they showed the potential for learning and leading and accomplishing their big ideas!

BE IDEA FRIENDLY: GATHER YOUR CROWD, BUILD CONNECTIONS, TAKE SMALL STEPS

Have you met everyone in town? Probably not! What are some ways you can bring people together to talk, learn from each other, see who might be interested in taking some small steps with you? Don't hold a meeting or go to city hall, go outside!

CHECK IN:

- What connections did you build?
- What worked and what didn't?
- What small step will you/your crowd take and when?

Finally, Focus on Your Assets

Leave the committee of negativity alone – they won't help you, anyway. Start by talking to people like you – who want to save your towns! You'll hear lots of ideas, and you want to encourage all the ideas! So, what if one or two fail? It's just a test of what works and what doesn't.

CARRY YOUR POSITIVE ATTITUDE FORWARD – DON'T BE DISMAYED. SHOW OFF WHAT YOU HAVE AND KEEP PEOPLE DREAMING.

WHAT ARE WAYS TO GET PEOPLE EXCITED ABOUT LIVING IN YOUR TOWN?

- **Highlight the unique features and attractions,** such as local festivals, historical landmarks, scenic views, and outdoor activities.
- **Mention the lower cost of living, fewer crowds, and less traffic** that can lead to a more relaxed and peaceful lifestyle.
- **Share success stories of people** who have found happiness and fulfillment living in your town.
- **Highlight the local cuisine and unique food options** that can only be found in the town. This can include mom-and-pop restaurants, farmers markets, and local bakeries.
- **Mention the benefits of a slower pace of life,** such as reduced stress levels and more time for hobbies and leisure activities.
- **Showcase the local schools and educational opportunities,** including smaller class sizes and more personalized attention from teachers.
- **Emphasize the sense of safety and security** that comes with living in a close-knit community.
- **Share stories of individuals who have made a meaningful impact,** whether through volunteer work, community activism, or other types of service.
- **Ignore the Committee of Negativity.**

PEOPLE, SCHOOLS, ARTISTS ARE ASSETS YOUR TOWN HAS.
WHAT ARE THE OTHER ASSETS?

- **Natural resources** such as scenic landscapes, babbling brooks, rapid waterfalls, old fishing holes, trails, big rocks out in the middle of a field that tell you a glacier has gone through. Everything has a story.
- **Historical landmarks** on signs, poles, fences, maps, and more. Tell those stories!
- **Quirky items** like the largest popcorn ball in Sac City, Iowa, for example. Santa Anna's wooden leg in Springfield, Illinois. The death certificate of the Wicked Witch of the West in Wamego, Kansas. You get the idea!
- **Recreational areas** for baseball, softball, soccer, basketball, pickleball and other areas for sports. Trails for walkers, bikers, fat tire bikers, four-wheelers, explorers and more.
- **Community events** – Oktoberfest in the Amana Colonies, Iowa. Underwater Music Festival – Looe Key, Florida. The Great Outhouse Races – Sapphire, North Carolina. Lumberjack World Championships – Hayward, Wisconsin.
- **Unique products and services** that showcase the town's character and charm.

BE IDEA FRIENDLY: GATHER YOUR CROWD, BUILD CONNECTIONS, TAKE SMALL STEPS

Take this worksheet and begin a list of the assets in your community. Post it and ask for input. Get people talking about the good things. Then make it into art. A poster, a flier, an article, an email … share it everywhere (send it to me, too.) Remind people why they live there.

Use these secrets in your town.

I COULD TELL YOU SO MANY MORE STORIES ABOUT COMMUNITIES I HAVE VISITED! There was this giant fish – I just had to have someone take our picture!. Be like me and take lots of pictures! Share them everywhere, because they tell the story of your town, too. I remember when they played human foosball in an Iowa event I helped organize. One night, I stayed in a haunted hotel. Another time, I learned how to be a licensed pyrotechnician. I still have that certificate!

THERE ARE MANY STORIES I HOLD DEAR
TO MY HEART, FROM TOWNS JUST
LIKE YOURS. SMALL,
RURAL COMMUNITIES.

There is magic in your town.

In the smallest steps people take. In the history of your brave pioneers. In the future of your children. If you don't tell your stories, share your experiences with the world and shout from the rooftops of all the miraculous things in your town – who will? You can create the future of your small town.

Stop waiting on some unknown business, foundation or person to come save you. You already have everything you need.

IN CLOSING, THANK YOU FOR BUYING THIS BOOK AND SHARING IT WITH YOUR COMMUNITY IN THE ACTIONS YOU TAKE. SOME PARTING ADVICE:

DON'T DO IT ALONE. ONE OF THE BENEFITS OF LIVING IN A SMALL TOWN IS THERE ARE PEOPLE YOU KNOW THAT WANT TO HELP YOU. TRY YOUR IDEA WITH A CROWD OF PEOPLE. MAKE PLANS WHERE EVERYONE CAN CONTRIBUTE. HAVE FUN, LAUGH A LOT AND BE THE PERSON YOU WANT TO LIVE IN YOUR SMALL TOWN.

THANKS,

~ Deb Brown

DEB@SAVEYOUR.TOWN

But wait, there's more...

Dig Deep Bonus
LATER HOURS

Things are changing for retailers, and one of those changes is keeping the store open later. Many parents work and are not able to shop if your store isn't open. Shopping online has become easier for them.

WHY STAY OPEN LATE?
- **Attract customers who work during the day** or have other obligations.
- **Compete with larger retailers** in nearby cities that have longer operating hours.
- **Cater to tourists or travelers** passing through the area who may not have time to shop during regular business hours.
- **Drive foot traffic and increase sales** by hosting special events or promotions during extended operating hours.

DR. SCOTT DAKO, FROM WARWICK BUSINESS SCHOOL, TALKS ABOUT "TIME OF DAY" AND SHARES SOME OF HIS RESEARCH. LET'S LOOK AT WHO SHOPS WHEN:

- Mornings: Older people, unemployed, "non-time pressured" people, "variety-seekers and families with small children".
- Afternoons: Youngsters and young adults, people looking for a new experience, those without "time-pressure" and who have no small children.
- Evenings: Busy, "time-pressured" people.

Succeeding in evening hours is more like starting a whole new store targeting different customers and offering different merchandise in different ways. Becky McCray talks more about this at her Small Biz Survival site.

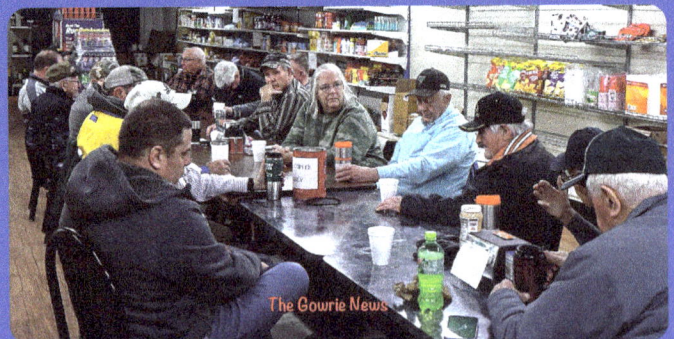

In Gowrie, Iowa, population 939, the grocery store is open early and late. In the morning, people gather in the back room for coffee and important discussions.

Can it work?

YES, IT CAN. IT WILL TAKE SOME WORK ON YOUR PART. TAKE A LOOK AT:

Who is your market, what do you know about your customers?

Different Times of Day Mean Different Customers. This could very well be the most valuable insight into small retail, ever. When do your customers shop? Most Point-of-Sale systems can show you what your busiest hours are. Look at those numbers for a three-month period. Now, you've got a better idea when you're seeing most of your business.

People shopping at different times even have different mindsets, Dako found. Daytime shoppers "tend to be more conscientious and agreeable". Evening shoppers "are more creative and flexible."

You can use this insight to set hours by deciding which groups are less important to your business. Think you don't need busy time-pressured people (that is, people with jobs and money)? Cut off evening hours. Or turn it around and decide which hours to be open to reach more different groups. Since small towns have a limited population, knowing how to reach additional groups may be the key to improving your chances for success.

Show them they're special.

When you know what new items you'll be offering for the evening customers, you don't want to sprinkle them throughout the store. That makes it hard for them to find. You have to show your new customers how they matter to you with a special display of stuff they'll love as soon as they walk in.

Can you make a quick-change display? How about a fancy wheelbarrow full of special evening items you can roll out at 6 p.m.? Maybe a special sidewalk display, created with help from a member of that target evening demographic.

ARE YOUR EVENING SHOPPERS A BIT HUNGRY? PUT OUT TREATS!

Can it work? CONTINUED

Share your expertise.

Kevin is a designer at his business Interior Spaces, in Webster City, Iowa, and he partners with a non-profit Legacy Learning Boone River Valley that provides art and nature workshops. Kevin teaches how to make a beautiful wreath for the holidays. The workshop is right in his store, and attendees can purchase more decorations for their wreaths as well. What could you teach at your business?

What kind of experience could you offer? Clothing stores could do fashion shows. Partner with artists in your town. Could someone come play a guitar and sing for a couple of hours? Offer workshops that showcase your products in your slow times.

THERE ARE A COUPLE OF SOLUTIONS.

You tell us you can't work that many hours.

- **Change your hours.**
  Do you need to be open at 9 am? Why not 11 to 7 instead?
- **Hire someone who will work the later hours.** Just because you don't like to work in the evening doesn't mean no one does. A stay-at-home parent may want a little income. A student might like to have those hours.
- **PopUps.** Who can set up a apop up in a corner and help man the store?
- **Skip the weekdays and focus on the weekends.** Juniper and Olive in Jewel, Iowa, is only open Saturday and Sunday from 11 a.m. to 4 p.m. Both owners work day jobs and they noticed there isn't much to do on the weekends in town. They serve food and cocktails and are extremely busy on Sundays! Several other merchants are now also open on Sunday afternoons. Jewel's retailers work together and take advantage of the opportunities available.

Worried about untrustworthy staff?

- **Get a surety bond** for only about $50 per hire that covers employee theft, among other things.
- **Install cameras.**
- **Create good inventory solutions.** How do you track your inventory now? There are many Point of Sales solutions that also track inventory. Reach out to other businesses and see what they use.

Finally...

- **Be consistent** as much as possible. If it's always changing, no one can get used to it.
- **Choose later hours as often and regularly as you can.** If Third Thursdays are a thing in your town, always be open that Thursday. I'd recommend being open late every Thursday. And try this experiment for at least a year. It takes time for customers to really believe you are open later.
- **Be open when you say you will.** Open on time, and don't close early.

Let's talk marketing

- **Don't go it alone.**
  Work with other businesses. In Tionesta, Pennsylvania, the Tionesta Market Village is open late, so the art gallery in town started staying open late too.

- **Try Dinner and a movie** kind of ideas. Can your restaurant and movie theater partner together on a promotion? What about the gym – try a workout and a healthy snack or smoothie afterwards? . If the library is open late, partner with them to talk about books and they can share places to buy a book bag.

MARKET IT.

UPDATE YOUR HOURS ONLINE, EVERYWHERE. CREATE A MARKETING CAMPAIGN AROUND THE NEW HOURS.

ADVERTISE.

- Use the **ways you already know** that work for you.

- **Try new ways** to spread the word too. Are you on Instagram? Or TikTok? Different types of customers use these platforms. Don't always rely on just one form of social media.

- **Add pictures** on a regular schedule to your Google Business listing.

- **Keep your website updated**. You own the content on your website. It's smart to direct people to the site for more details.

MAKE IT OBVIOUS YOU ARE OPEN.

ADD LIGHTS SO IT'S CLEAR YOU'RE OPEN AND PEOPLE FEEL SAFE. USE A SANDWICH BOARD WITH YOUR HOURS ON IT. PUT YOUR HOURS BIG AND BOLD WHERE PEOPLE CAN SEE THEM.

Photo by Becky McCray

Success Story | HUTCHINSON, KANSAS | POPULATION 39,699

Hutchinson invited a group of us to a bloggers tour. On Thursdays their stores are open late. Third Thursdays there turn into a celebration of local art, music, and community. They invite artists and musicians to set up in their stores, or in front of their stores, and the public comes out in full force to support the community. The picture is from one of my visits there.

BE IDEA FRIENDLY: GATHER YOUR CROWD, BUILD CONNECTIONS, TAKE SMALL STEPS

In Belle Plaine, Iowa, population 2,326, the mayor wanted to support later hours, so he set the example by keeping city hall open until 8 pm on Thursdays. What other businesses are already open late in your town/county? Are there businesses that could partner with artists and host workshops of some sort? I know of a hardware store that taught how to use chalk paint, for example.

CHECK IN:

- What connections did you build?
- What worked and what didn't?
- What small step will you/your crowd take and when?

Links:

- The mayor in Belle Plaine keeps city hall open later story:
  https://www.facebook.com/places/Things-to-do-in-Belle-Plaine-Iowa/108232835864284/
- Time of Day Marketing by Scott Dako:
  https://www.wbs.ac.uk/news/time-of-day-marketing-could-boost-high-street/
- How to draw customers into your store later story:
  https://smallbizsurvival.com/2014/05/how-to-draw-customers-to-your-store-for-evening-hours.html

Add an EV Station in Your Town

Success Story | RURAL PORTUGAL | POPULATION 3.3 MILLION

At a 3 Day Community Engagement in Grayson, Kentucky, we walked around downtown and I noticed a huge, mostly empty, parking lot. We had already talked about ways to get traffic off the highway and into downtown. Here was another idea they could try. Make a station for travelers in electric vehicles to recharge their vehicles! There could be an information kiosk with places to visit, or map of the stores downtown. It would also bring in extra income to the city/county. Win-win.

These two gentlemen are friends of mine who live in Portugal. Note that 32% of Portugal's population is rural. We visited small towns, and there are EV stations all over the countryside. They've placed them near restaurants and shopping locations, and along the roads in desolate areas.

ELECTRIC VEHICLES ALREADY ARE IN USE, AND YOUR TOURISTS ARE DRIVING THEM. WHY NOT PROVIDE RESOURCES THEY NEED?

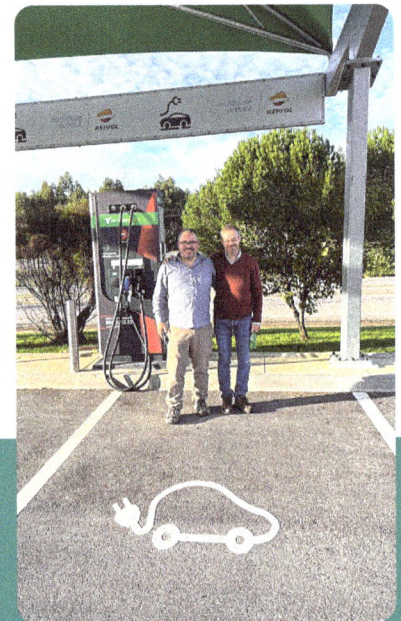

WHY SHOULD YOU HAVE EV STATIONS?

- **Encourages the adoption of electric vehicles,** more people will be willing to purchase electric vehicles, knowing that they can easily find a place to charge their car.

- **Increases property values:** small towns that have EV stations are likely to attract more environmentally conscious homebuyers, which can increase property values in the area.

- **Helps reduce air pollution:** By offering an alternative to gas-powered cars, a town with EV stations can help reduce air pollution and improve air quality.

- **Supports local businesses:** EV owners typically spend more time and money in the areas where they can charge their cars. Tourists will find you on Google Maps. This means that a town with EV stations can benefit from increased foot traffic and support for local businesses.

- **Be forward thinking:** having EV stations in town helps to contribute to the mindset your town is forward-thinking. Another way to help create that mindset is to rent out your home EV charger. You can start smaller and simply rent out your home EV charger. No kidding. There are apps for this, it's like an AirBnB for your car!

BE IDEA FRIENDLY: GATHER YOUR CROWD, BUILD CONNECTIONS, TAKE SMALL STEPS

Start talking about EV stations, about how they might help bring in more tourists. Someone can take a look at federal funding that is available for transportation (and there's quite a bit of it.) Reach out to your representatives and ask what they are doing about this topic. Hold them to task.

_____

_____

_____

_____

_____

_____

_____

_____

_____

_____

_____

_____

CHECK IN:

What connections did you build? What worked and what didn't?
What small step will you/your crowd take and when?

_____

_____

_____

_____

_____

It's a Snowball Effect

ENTREPRENEURS WORKING TOGETHER

It is common in Latino culture for one entrepreneur to connect with and extend opportunities to more people from their community. This is the story of expanding, diverse businesses in Webster City, Iowa.

INCUBATOR PROGRAM CAME FIRST

Diana Castro started a business in Webster City, Iowa, by taking advantage of a reduced rent incubator program. Diana and her team carried youth clothing, shoes, hats and caps and miscellaneous Chicago and Hispanic labeled products in the incubator space.

NEXT WAS A LARGER BUILDING AND ROOM FOR MORE

They did well and went on to purchase a larger building in the same block. They expanded their lines, and opened up a couple of spaces in the building for others to try their ideas out.

ONE OF THE MOST SUCCESSFUL SPACES THAT HER DAUGHTER LAURA OPENED IS A SMALL ICE CREAM SHOP WITH FROZEN TREATS AND DRINKS.

They went on to add simple Mexican food for lunch. Diana's husband is rehabbing other empty spaces in the building's first floor. Eventually they will fix the second floor for possible housing.

THE FLOODGATES OPENED: GROCERIES, BARBERS, CLOTHING

DIANA'S SUCCESS CAUSED AN INFLUX OF BIZ.

Two doors down another Hispanic local opened up a small grocery store, El Mercadito Tienda Mexicana. They found out they didn't need a large inventory of food so they shrunk the food footprint, and added other items like bedding.

A young barber, Eddie, from a neighboring town, realized his clientele were mostly from Webster City. So he rented a space across the street from Diana's and has one chair there.

Eddie's boss from the other town decided to relocate to Webster City too. He rented a larger building, and only has one chair in it. But he's also made it a third space by adding a pool table, sofas and soft drink machines. There's room to grow too.

The empty place right next to him is now a second-hand clothing store and always busy. They also have quite the knack for exciting window displays that draw in all types of customers.

ONE RESTAURANT CLOSED AND NEW OWNERS TOOK OVER

The owners of a beloved restaurant in the same block, Second Street Emporium, retired. A young Hispanic family, Armando, Isabel and Tomas Solis, and Ignacio Gonzalez and Georgina Santiago, are leasing the space, and still serving the same food. They are on a learning curve and working hard to adjust to different styles of food and cooking.

GOT TO HAVE ART!

DIANA ALSO MADE THE BOARDED UP WINDOWS ON THE SECOND FLOOR AVAILABLE FOR THE COMMUNITY TO USE AS AN ART PROJECT. EACH WINDOW HAD A MURAL PAINTED ON IT THAT REPRESENTED SIGNIFICANT COMMUNITY FEATURES AND HISTORICAL FIGURES.

The murals, seen elsewhere in the book, were funded through a grant partnership between the City of Webster City and the University of Iowa. Diana only requested that one window had a dove on it – a symbol of Hope and peace for the future of Webster City and its residents.

WHAT'S THE LESSONS LEARNED?

There are a couple of interesting things happening here. The Hispanic market is growing! As is the Hispanic population. I talked with a couple of the other business owners in the block and they made some observations.

• The Hispanic population is not as risk averse as the rest of the population in town.

HISPANIC BUSINESSES ARE TRYING THEIR IDEAS OUT AND ADJUSTING IF THEY AREN'T WORKING.

• Other entrepreneurs in town are catching on. One young gentleman, Brady, has built a building on an empty lot and has room for three retail/service spots. Two young hairdressers are going into one of the spots. He's actively looking for entrepreneurs who have a home-based business to try out one of the other spots.

• The Hispanic businesses have set their open hours primarily from noon to 9 p.m. The rest of the businesses in the block are open 9 to 5. Hispanics are first catering to the hours their people can shop. Mothers shop after lunch. Many work late and need later hours. The bonus for them is they are seeing more people from the community come in the evening, too.

• The other barber and the third space is giving a place for the Hispanic men to gather. In the places they are from, socializing in the street is normal and accepted. In rural Iowa, not so much.

BE IDEA FRIENDLY: GATHER YOUR CROWD, BUILD CONNECTIONS, TAKE SMALL STEPS

What do we have to learn from each other as people from different backgrounds and cultures? Many people are happy to be invited to the party as they celebrate special events and share traditional foods. How can new opportunities be created – social, business and recreational in your small town? Where will you go to meet people to talk with about this?

CHECK IN:

What connections did you build? What worked and what didn't?
What small step will you/your crowd take and when?

A Gift For You

Idea Friendly Method Toolkit

Because you
purchased this book, you will receive
access, for free, to our Idea Friendly Method Toolkit!

ARE YOU READY TO USE THE IDEA FRIENDLY METHOD
IN YOUR COMMUNITY? READY TO REACH MORE PEOPLE, BUT
NEED TO GET THEM UP TO SPEED? NEED A CERTIFICATE
TO SHOW YOUR PROGRESS? OUR NEW IDEA FRIENDLY
METHOD TOOLKIT MAKES IT EASY!

Here's what I need you to do. Answer these questions and send the answers in
an email to deb@saveyour.town I will send you the link after I receive your answers!

- Your name and where you live
- Where you purchased the book. If it's an independent bookstore,
  let me know the name and city please.
- What is your big idea?
- What will be your first small step?

Thanks | Deb

P.S. If you're not receiving our weekly newsletters please
sign up at https://saveyour.town/signup

Book Club Discussion Guide

HERE IS A SECTION DESIGNED FOR BOOK CLUBS TO DISCUSS "FROM POSSIBILITIES TO REALITY: SAVE YOUR SMALL TOWN WITH THESE UNIQUELY DO-ABLE IDEAS, PROJECTS, AND SUCCESS STORIES."

This book provides a wealth of inspiring stories and practical ideas for revitalizing small towns. Here are some questions to guide your book club's discussion:

1. Which story or example from the book resonated with you the most? What made it interesting and you want to take action on it?

2. The Idea Friendly Method is a core concept – gather your crowd, build connections, and take small steps. Discuss a situation where you could apply this method in your own community. What would be your "big idea" to start with?

3. Several chapters highlight the importance of promoting and marketing your town's assets and events. What are some quiet gems in your community that could be better showcased?

4. The book emphasizes involving and engaging the entire community, from youth to seniors. How could you facilitate more conversations between youth and seniors?

5. Discuss public spaces, art, and placemaking ideas that would help create more community pride and attachment. What opportunities exist in your town for creative placemaking projects?

6. Many examples illustrate repurposing vacant buildings and lots. What kind of empty spaces do you have in your town? What could you do with them?

7. The book stresses the importance of celebrating your town's unique history and culture. What would you like to celebrate in your town?

8. Several stories highlight successful fundraising efforts for community projects. What fundraising strategies or events could work well in your town?

9. Discuss the challenges of rural brain drain and engaging youth. What initiatives could help in your community?

10. After reading the book, what is one concrete action step or small project you want to take? Who will you ask to help?

By exploring these questions, your book club can

REFLECT ON THE LESSONS FROM THE BOOK

and brainstorm ways to apply them to strengthen your own community's future.

DEB BROWN HAS LIVED THROUGH ALL THIS ~ AND SEEN HER TOWN AND OTHERS EMERGE STRONGER

This book is for anyone who lives or works in a small rural town. Many of our rural towns are struggling, whether due to a large industrial employer moving away, or any of the other economic and social changes that have rocked small communities, leaving people to wonder what the future looks like.

Deb Brown has lived through all this – and helped her town and others emerge stronger. No matter who you are, you have the power to improve your community—and you'll be surprised how many people are willing to help. This book is designed to help you get organized and start making meaningful changes that will keep your community alive and make it a better place to live for everyone.

You'll learn the Idea Friendly Method. Hear stories of small towns and their success stories. And learn about easy-to-do projects you can help get started in your town. Hundreds of tried-and-true ideas lie inside these covers. So, choose your big idea, gather your crowd, and take small steps... and your vision for your town will move from possibilities to reality!

There is magic in your town. In the smallest steps people take. In the history of your brave pioneers. In the future of your children. If you don't tell your stories, share your experiences with the world and shout from the rooftops of all the miraculous things in your town - who will? You choose how you see and create the future of your small town.

Stop waiting on some unknown business/entity/ person to come save you. You already have everything you need.

Take action now.

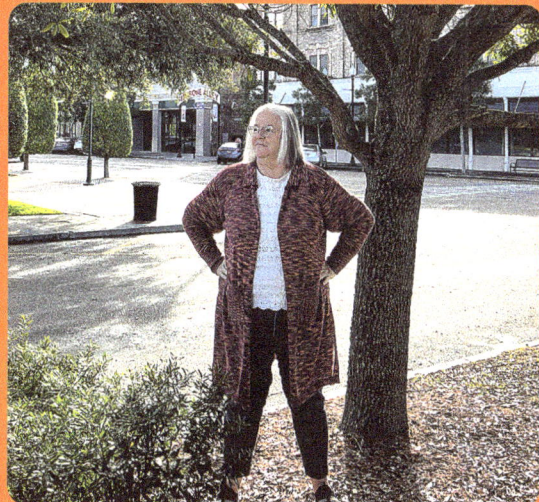

ADDITIONAL NOTES:

www.ingramcontent.com/pod-product-compliance
Lightning Source LLC
Chambersburg PA
CBHW061224270326
41927CB00025B/3485